This Book Belongs To:
Mrs. Bartsch

DOUGAL DIXON'S
DINOSAURS

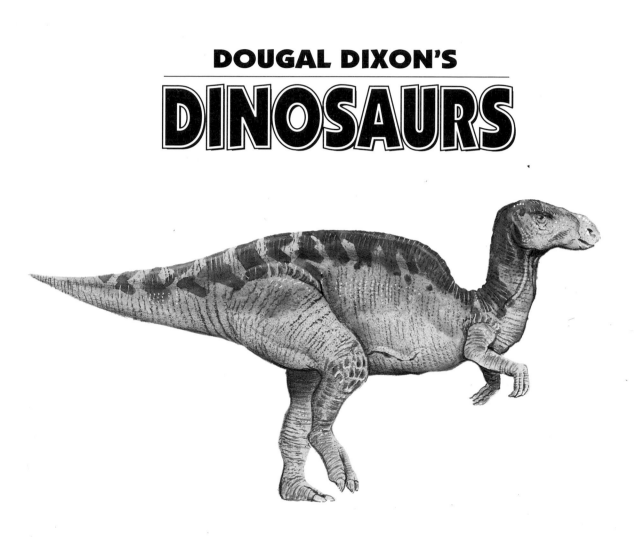

The author wishes to express his gratitude to the following scientists whose valuable contributions made the book possible:

Peter Dodson, consultant on *Dougal Dixon's Dinosaurs*, is professor of anatomy at the School of Veterinary Medicine and adjunct professor of geology at the University of Pennsylvania in Philadelphia. He is also a research associate at the Academy of Natural Sciences in Philadelphia. He has collected fossils in the Canadian Arctic as well as in western Canada and the United States for many years. In 1986 he described a new horned dinosaur, *Avaceratops lammersi*, that he collected in Montana.

Jack Myers, Ph.D., editor of *Dougal Dixon's Dinosaurs*, is the science editor of *Highlights for Children*. He is also professor emeritus of zoology and botany at the University of Texas in Austin and a member of the National Academy of Sciences. Jack Myers's love for science is based on exploring and describing how things work in nature, and in his writing and editing Jack Myers treats science as the ongoing search for understanding of the nature of our world.

The Dinosaur Society is an international, non-profit corporation that financially supports paleontological research and education. For information write to The Dinosaur Society, 200 Carleton Avenue, East Islip, New York 11730.

Published by Bell Books
Boyds Mills Press, Inc.
A Highlights Company
815 Church Street
Honesdale, Pennsylvania 18431
Printed in Spain

Publisher Cataloging-in-Publication Data
Dixon, Dougal.
    Dougal Dixon's dinosaurs / by Dougal Dixon.—1st ed.
[160]p. : col. ill. ; cm.
Includes index and maps.
Summary: The life and times of dinosaurs, from their evolution to the present-day discovery of their fossils.
ISBN 1-56397-261-1
1. Dinosaurs—Juvenile literature. 2. Paleontology—Juvenile literature.
[1. Dinosaurs. 2. Paleontology.] I. Title.
567.9 / 1—dc20   1993   CIP
Library of Congress Catalog Card Number: 92-76174

First edition, 1993
Book designed and produced by Bender Richardson White

10 9 8 7 6 5 4 3 2 1

On page 3: Velociraptor, a small dinosaur that could run as fast as a racehorse.

DOUGAL DIXON'S
DINOSAURS

By Dougal Dixon

MORENA PRESS

CONTENTS

About this book
The dinosaurs were among the most successful and most magnificent animals that have ever lived. We cannot think of them as failures just because they do not happen to be around any more. They lived from about 225 million years ago up to 65 million years ago. A history of 160 million years of survival is hardly one of failure! Especially when we consider that our own successful human species has been around for 250,000 years at the most.

The term *dinosaur* comes from scientific words meaning "terrible lizard." Some dinosaurs were indeed fierce animals and did look like present-day lizards. But others resembled different kinds of reptiles, such as crocodiles, or mammals and birds.

Dougal Dixon's Dinosaurs starts with the history of life on Earth prior to the dinosaurs. The survey of dinosaurs forming the core of the book looks in detail at more than 25 different kinds. The book ends with the discovery of dinosaurs and the ongoing search for a precise picture of how they lived and died.

The book is divided into chapters and double-page spreads. Each spread is a complete story. So you can either read through the book from beginning to end, or just dip into it to learn about a specific dinosaur or topic. Do You Know? (pages 146-150) includes some of the more interesting and amazing facts and figures about dinosaurs. The Glossary (pages 151-156) explains scientific and technical terms used in the book.

The Age of Dinosaurs

The first dinosaurs appeared about 225 million years ago (mya for short) in what scientists call the Late Triassic Period. They thrived through the following Jurassic Period and died out at the end of the Cretaceous Period 65 million years ago. During this time, geography, climate, and vegetation, or plant life, were constantly changing—as shown in these dinosaur scenes.

Triassic 245–208 mya
A single giant landmass or supercontinent, mostly desert conditions, tree ferns, and conifers.

Early and Middle Jurassic 208–157 mya Supercontinent, shallow seas, moist climate, tree ferns, conifers, and cycads.

ONE

Giants of the Earth

When we look at a dinosaur skeleton in a museum, at a dinosaur model in a display, or at a dinosaur picture in a book, we are at first amazed by the strangeness of the creature. We wonder that such an incredible beast could exist at all. Then, when we begin to read about dinosaurs, and to understand them and how they lived, we begin to ask questions.

Where did the dinosaurs come from? What kind of world did they live in? How long did they exist?

These are all questions that scientists have been trying to answer for more than 160 years. Some answers to them come from the rocks in which dinosaur bones are found. The kinds of rocks can tell us about the landscapes of the past—for instance, sandstones that formed in huge ancient deserts, shale and mudstones from deep, wide, muddy rivers,

and limestones that formed in lime-rich seas millions of years ago.

The remains of living creatures that we find in the rocks are called fossils, and these can tell us about the dinosaurs' surroundings. Plant fossils show us the vegetation, and animal fossils show us the other creatures that lived at the same time.

The fossils from rocks dating from before the Age of Dinosaurs can give us a picture of life on Earth up to that time. We can work out the evolution of the dinosaurs from the different kinds of animals that existed earlier.

We still do not have all the answers about dinosaurs, and every fresh discovery tells us something new. However, slowly over the years we have been building up a picture of these magnificent creatures of the past, and of their world.

Late Jurassic 157–146 mya
Supercontinent beginning to break up, dry inland, moist climates by coasts.

Early Cretaceous 146–97 mya
Continents drifting into separate landmasses, plant life as in Triassic and Jurassic periods.

Late Cretaceous 97–65 mya
Separate continents, each with its own animal life, and plants like modern types.

DINOSAUR PARADE BEGINS

Here they come! A parade of the animals that lived on Earth between the Late Triassic Period, about 225 million years ago, and the end of the Cretaceous Period, about 65 million years ago.

At the beginning, in the Triassic, there were all kinds of reptiles—running reptiles, swimming reptiles, digging reptiles, even flying reptiles. (There were also the first mammals. Those were small, shrewlike animals.) Among the reptiles were some crocodile-like animals, each with a long tail and strong hind legs. Scientists call these creatures the thecodonts. They became great in number when the other types of reptiles died out, and their descendants—the animals that evolved from them—took up many kinds of lifestyles. As they did so, they developed bodily shapes to suit their behavior. One group of thecodonts began to walk about on their strong hind legs, holding their long tails out behind them to balance. These animals became the first dinosaurs. The earliest dinosaurs were nimble little hunting animals not much different from their thecodont ancestors, the creatures they evolved from.

▷ In the parade of Triassic and Early Jurassic animals we can see the first of the dinosaurs emerging. These included meat- eaters like *Staurikosaurus* and *Coelophysis*, long-necked plant-eaters like *Anchisaurus* and *Plateosaurus*, and two-footed plant-eaters— those that moved around on just their hind legs— like *Fabrosaurus* and *Heterodontosaurus*.

Kuehneosaurus

Erythrosuchus

Hyperodapedon

Stagonolepis

Rutiodon

Cynognathus

Lystrosaurus

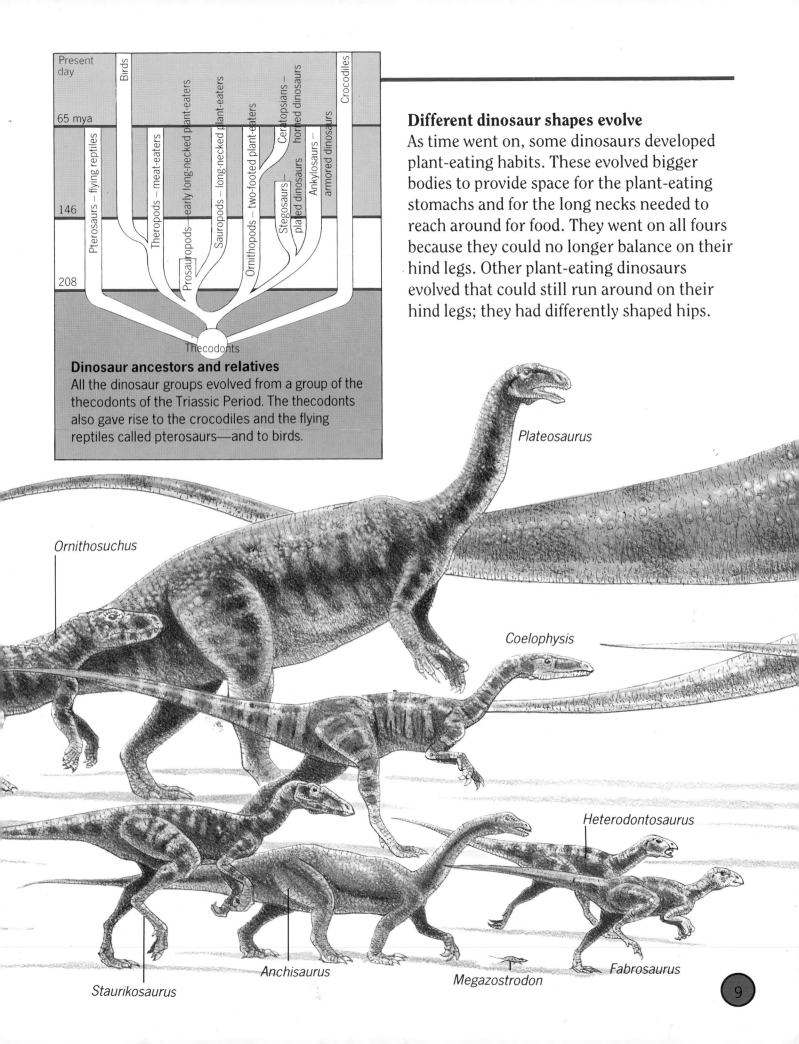

Present day								
65 mya								
146								
208								

Birds

Pterosaurs – flying reptiles

Theropods – meat-eaters

Prosauropods – early long-necked plant-eaters

Sauropods – long-necked plant-eaters

Ornithopods – two-footed plant-eaters

Stegosaurs – plated dinosaurs

Ceratopsians – horned dinosaurs

Ankylosaurs – armored dinosaurs

Crocodiles

Thecodonts

Dinosaur ancestors and relatives
All the dinosaur groups evolved from a group of the thecodonts of the Triassic Period. The thecodonts also gave rise to the crocodiles and the flying reptiles called pterosaurs—and to birds.

Different dinosaur shapes evolve
As time went on, some dinosaurs developed plant-eating habits. These evolved bigger bodies to provide space for the plant-eating stomachs and for the long necks needed to reach around for food. They went on all fours because they could no longer balance on their hind legs. Other plant-eating dinosaurs evolved that could still run around on their hind legs; they had differently shaped hips.

Plateosaurus

Coelophysis

Ornithosuchus

Heterodontosaurus

Staurikosaurus

Anchisaurus

Megazostrodon

Fabrosaurus

9

DINOSAURS MARCH ON

The parade of dinosaurs continues in the Jurassic Period. This was the greatest time of the dinosaurs. The desert conditions of the Triassic gave way to moister climates in the Jurassic as shallow seas spread over the continents. All sorts of new dinosaurs evolved to live in the woodlands and forests of the new environments.

The swift-moving little meat-eaters were still around, but there were also huge, dragonlike meat-eaters. These great killers evolved to feed upon the plant-eaters that had also grown huge. The long-necked four-footed plant-eaters were the largest land animals that ever lived. The two-footed plant-eaters continued, too, and some of these developed into armored types—great heavy beasts that also had gone back to a four-footed way of life.

The skies were dominated by the flying reptiles, the pterosaurs, but the true birds evolved at the end of the Jurassic Period. The small mammals still scuttled around, but had not developed into any particularly special creatures.

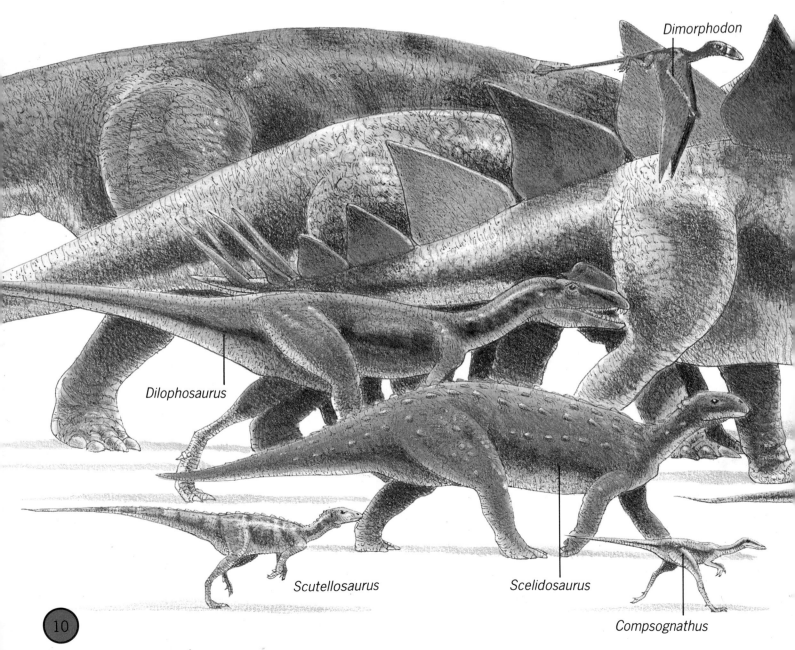

Dimorphodon

Dilophosaurus

Scutellosaurus

Scelidosaurus

Compsognathus

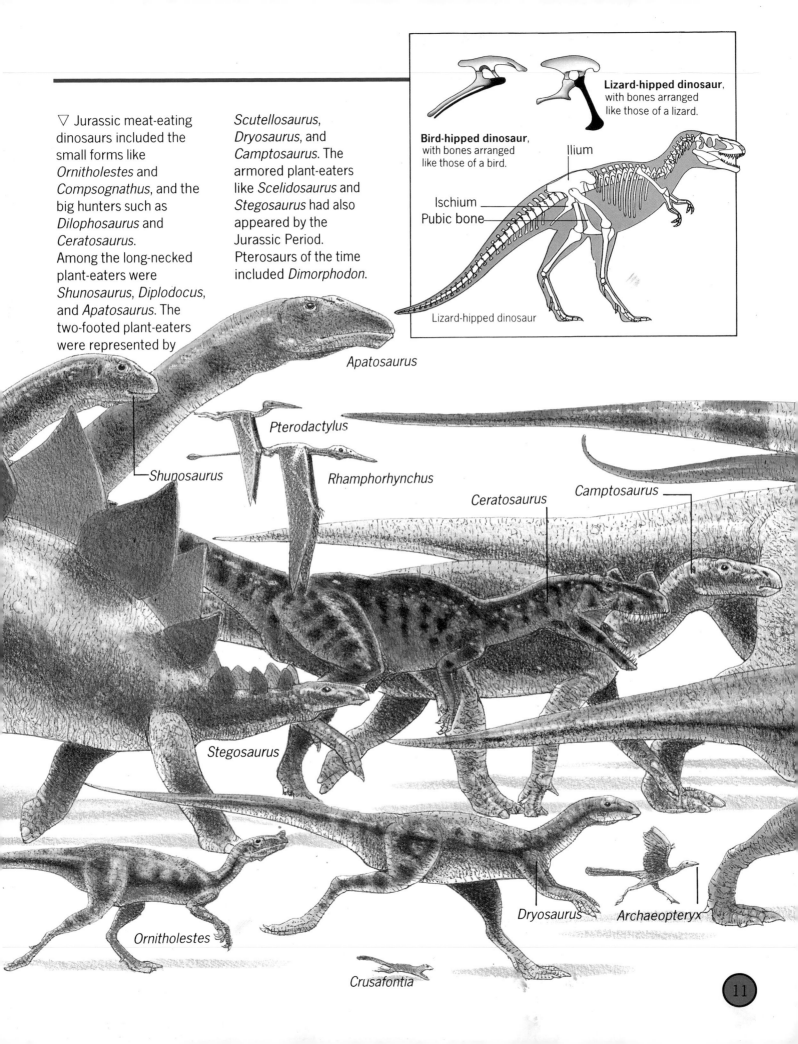

▽ Jurassic meat-eating dinosaurs included the small forms like *Ornitholestes* and *Compsognathus*, and the big hunters such as *Dilophosaurus* and *Ceratosaurus*. Among the long-necked plant-eaters were *Shunosaurus*, *Diplodocus*, and *Apatosaurus*. The two-footed plant-eaters were represented by *Scutellosaurus*, *Dryosaurus*, and *Camptosaurus*. The armored plant-eaters like *Scelidosaurus* and *Stegosaurus* had also appeared by the Jurassic Period. Pterosaurs of the time included *Dimorphodon*.

Bird-hipped dinosaur, with bones arranged like those of a bird.

Lizard-hipped dinosaur, with bones arranged like those of a lizard.

Ilium

Ischium

Pubic bone

Lizard-hipped dinosaur

Apatosaurus

Pterodactylus

Shunosaurus

Rhamphorhynchus

Ceratosaurus

Camptosaurus

Stegosaurus

Dryosaurus

Archaeopteryx

Ornitholestes

Crusafontia

11

DINOSAUR PARADE ENDS

By the time the parade arrives in the Cretaceous Period, it has reached the peak of dinosaur development. Along with the small and big meat-eaters, the long-necked and the two-footed plant-eaters, we also find new kinds of armored dinosaurs including bizarre horned types.

Up to this point the same types of dinosaurs had lived all over the world. Now we are seeing different types appearing on different continents. A type of two-footed plant-eater was widespread in North America, while the long-necked plant-eaters continued to be most important in South America.

Then, at the end of the Cretaceous, just as they were becoming really spectacular, the dinosaurs suddenly vanished. The parade came to a halt. And along with the dinosaurs went the pterosaurs and other great reptile types of the time. It was the little mammals that continued. So unimportant throughout the Age of Dinosaurs, they survived the reptiles and went on to produce their own parade that brings us up to the present day.

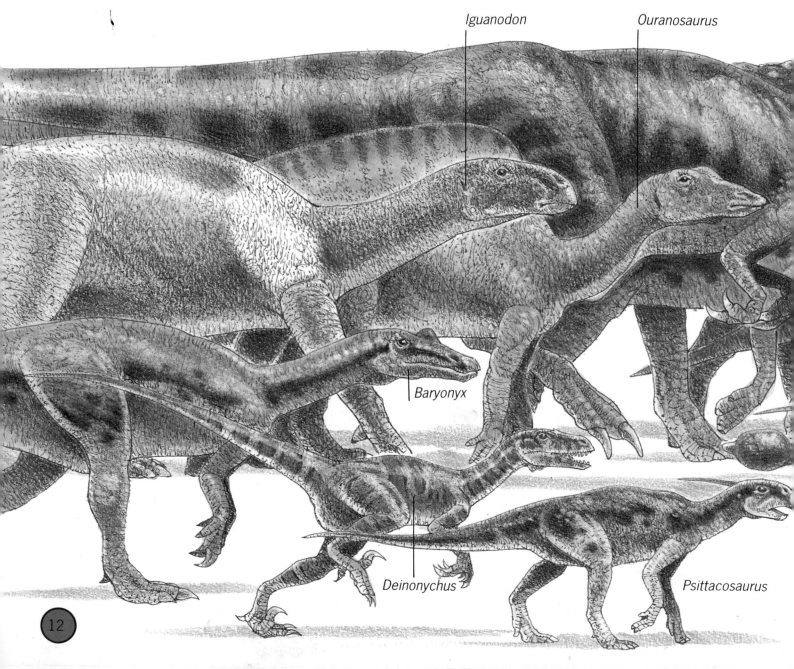

Iguanodon

Ouranosaurus

Baryonyx

Deinonychus

Psittacosaurus

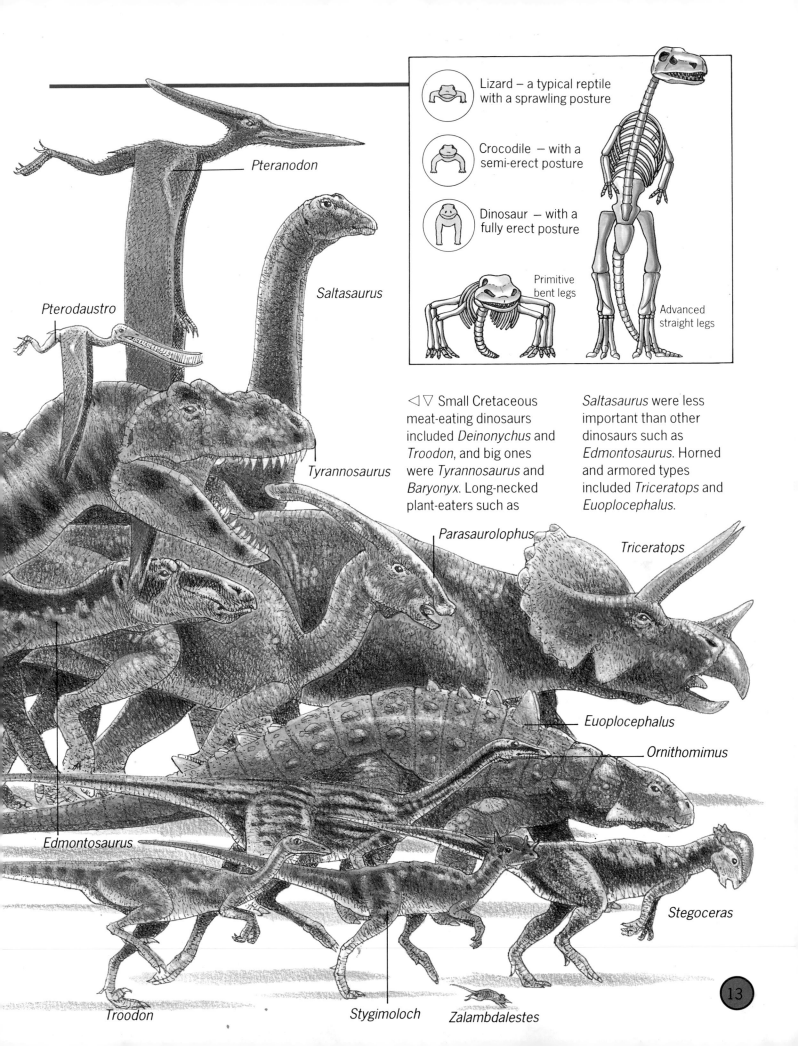

Pteranodon

Saltasaurus

Pterodaustro

Lizard – a typical reptile with a sprawling posture

Crocodile – with a semi-erect posture

Dinosaur – with a fully erect posture

Primitive bent legs

Advanced straight legs

◁▽ Small Cretaceous meat-eating dinosaurs included *Deinonychus* and *Troodon*, and big ones were *Tyrannosaurus* and *Baryonyx*. Long-necked plant-eaters such as

Saltasaurus were less important than other dinosaurs such as *Edmontosaurus*. Horned and armored types included *Triceratops* and *Euoplocephalus*.

Tyrannosaurus

Parasaurolophus

Triceratops

Euoplocephalus

Ornithomimus

Edmontosaurus

Stegoceras

Troodon

Stygimoloch

Zalambdalestes

THE TIME SCALE OF EVOLUTION

It has taken the Earth a long time to get to where it is today—about 4.6 thousand million years, in fact. At first the Earth was a ball of hot molten rock. Then it started to cool down. There have probably been living things of some sort present on Earth as long as its surface has been solid and cool enough to support them.

▽ The evolution of, or changes to, the surface of the Earth, from the time it started to cool until the present day. Each level of the folded band covers a little more than 1,000 million years.

At first, life forms would only have been made up of molecules of matter that could reproduce, or make copies of, themselves. Any change to these molecules that would have improved their chances of reproduction would be carried on to the next molecules: their offspring or children. Then the whole machinery of evolution would have been set in motion. Evolution is a process by which new kinds, or species, of living things develop from others.

These early forms of life left no remains, or fossils, and for about seven-eighths of the Earth's history we have only the vaguest idea of what types of living things were around.

Ice age

Mass extinction

First land animals

First land plants

First life

First oceans

Then, 570 million years ago, animals with hard shells evolved. These produced fossils. From that time we have a clearer picture of how life developed. At first all creatures lived in the sea. But about 420 million years ago, plants and animals began to grow on the land. Some fish left the water and evolved into amphibians, of which present-day frogs and toads are examples. From these, the reptiles evolved. The period of time between 245 and 65 million years ago is known as the Age of Reptiles. Within this period was the time of dinosaurs. When the big reptiles vanished, the Age of Mammals began, and this has lasted to the present day.

First hard-shelled animals

First traces of oxygen in atmosphere

Earth cooling

4,600
Precambrian

Geological periods

Geology is the study of the Earth's rocks. Geological time, the Earth's lifespan, is so long that scientists find it helpful to divide it up into sections called periods. Each period is marked by the kinds of animals that existed at that time, and hence on the fossils that we find in the rocks laid down then. The dinosaurs lived in the Age of Reptiles—the Triassic, Jurassic, and Cretaceous periods. [All dates in the chart are in millions of years ago.]

Holocene 0.01-0
Modern times.

Pleistocene 1.64-0.01
Ice-age mammals including early humans.

Pliocene 5.2-1.64
Cool climates. Mammal life similar to present day.

Miocene 23.5-5.2
Mountain ranges form. Widespread grass-eating, running mammals.

Oligocene 35.5-23.5
Cool climate. Mammals beginning to look like modern types.

Eocene 56.5-35.5
Forests. Mammals widespread.

Paleocene 65-56.5
Forests. All kinds of new mammals develop.

Cretaceous 146-65
Forests, then shallow seas. Last of the dinosaurs.

Jurassic 208-146
Shallow seas, wooded islands. First birds.

Triassic 245-208
Dry land with deserts. First dinosaurs and mammals.

Permian 290-245
Mountains and deserts. Reptiles dominate the land.

Carboniferous 363-290
Seas, swamps, then ice. First reptiles.

Devonian 409-363
Mountains and lakes. First amphibians.

Silurian 439-409
Ice caps over seas, then open seas. First land plants.

Ordovician 510-439
Dry land without plants, then seas. First fish.

Cambrian 570-510
Widespread seas. First shelled animals.

Precambrian 4,600-570
Shallow seas. Only simple life.

THE MOVING WORLD

360–286 mya
In the Carboniferous Period, most of the continents of the time (gray areas) were joined together, and the rest were drifting toward this great landmass.

245–208 mya
In the Triassic Period, when the dinosaurs first appeared, the continents were jammed together to form a supercontinent, called Pangaea.

208–146 mya
During the Jurassic Period, Pangaea was still one single continent, but it was beginning to split. Shallow seas flooded over much of it.

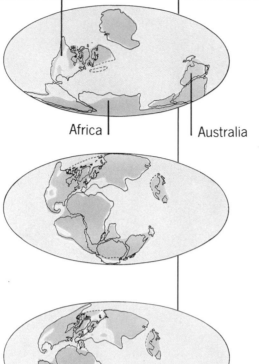

North America

Africa

Australia

We live, and the dinosaurs lived, in a world that is constantly changing.

The surface of the land is continually being worn away by the action of the rain, rivers, glaciers, wind, and all other kinds of natural processes. Over millions of years, mountains are worn down to rubble and sand, which are carried away by streams and rivers and dumped on plains and in oceans. There they form rocks, which can be folded up into new mountains and added to the continents.

Not only that, but the very structure of the continents is changing. And the continents are slowly moving about over the surface of the Earth. Our planet consists of a number of layers—the core, the mantle, and the crust. The crust and a solid part of the mantle below it form giant plates on the Earth's surface.

Structure of the Earth
The mantle forms the largest portion of the Earth. Movements in the mantle, in which molten rock material rises and spreads out and cool rock material sinks, are responsible for the movement of the Earth's outer layers. The top layer is called the crust. It is the Earth's skin.

Volcanoes

Coastal mountain range

Ocean plate sliding beneath continental plate

Ocean ridge

Margin where plate destroyed

Mantle material rising

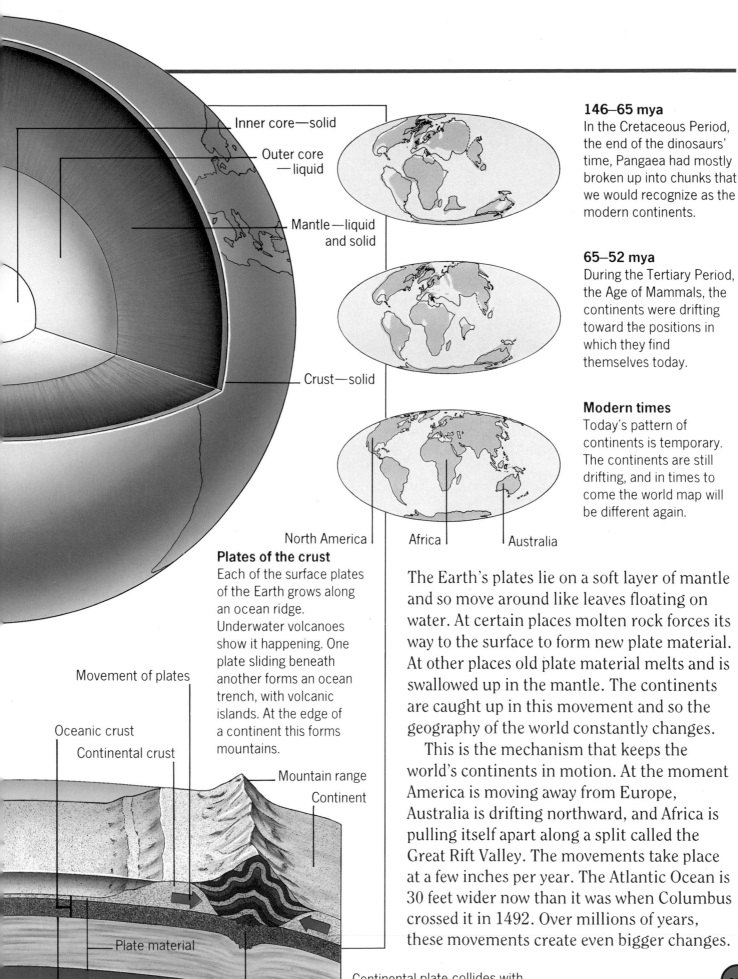

Inner core—solid

Outer core —liquid

Mantle—liquid and solid

Crust—solid

146–65 mya
In the Cretaceous Period, the end of the dinosaurs' time, Pangaea had mostly broken up into chunks that we would recognize as the modern continents.

65–52 mya
During the Tertiary Period, the Age of Mammals, the continents were drifting toward the positions in which they find themselves today.

Modern times
Today's pattern of continents is temporary. The continents are still drifting, and in times to come the world map will be different again.

North America   Africa   Australia

Plates of the crust
Each of the surface plates of the Earth grows along an ocean ridge. Underwater volcanoes show it happening. One plate sliding beneath another forms an ocean trench, with volcanic islands. At the edge of a continent this forms mountains.

The Earth's plates lie on a soft layer of mantle and so move around like leaves floating on water. At certain places molten rock forces its way to the surface to form new plate material. At other places old plate material melts and is swallowed up in the mantle. The continents are caught up in this movement and so the geography of the world constantly changes.

This is the mechanism that keeps the world's continents in motion. At the moment America is moving away from Europe, Australia is drifting northward, and Africa is pulling itself apart along a split called the Great Rift Valley. The movements take place at a few inches per year. The Atlantic Ocean is 30 feet wider now than it was when Columbus crossed it in 1492. Over millions of years, these movements create even bigger changes.

Movement of plates

Oceanic crust

Continental crust

Mountain range

Continent

Plate material

Mantle

Continental plate collides with continental plate

AT THE BEGINNING

The first part of the history of life on our planet—the time known as the Precambrian Era—is very unclear. All living things had soft bodies and left few fossils for us to study. Then, in the Cambrian Period, animals developed shells and horny coverings. These are the kinds of things we often find as fossils. We do not know why this change happened. Maybe the chemicals in the seawater changed and allowed animals to grow hard parts. Anyway, from the Cambrian Period onward, the rocks are full of fossils and we can trace the evolution of life with some confidence.

In telling the dinosaur story, two events were very important: the development of vertebrates, and the colonization of land. The first vertebrates—animals with backbones—were the fish. These evolved from wormlike creatures that had a stiff rod supporting a long body.

Early life forms
The first living creatures had just one cell. They must have resembled some modern blue-green algae. In modern waters mats of blue-green algae trap mud and build up lumps called stromatolites like the ones in this photo. Fossil stromatolites are known from Precambrian rocks.

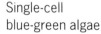

Single-cell blue-green algae

Cambrian Period 570–510 million years ago
The first common fossils are found in Cambrian rocks. These are of spongelike and wormlike sea creatures, and of the first animals with hard shells.

Ordovician Period 510–439 million years ago
The first fish evolved in the Ordovician Period, but the more common fossils are of lampshells, nautilus-like animals, trilobites, and sea lilies.

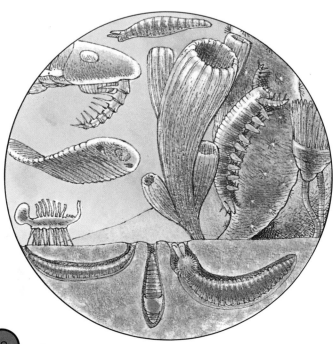

In the early fish, the stiff rod became divided into sections, making it flexible like a chain. Flaps evolved at each side of the body to allow swimming. And the brain at the front of the animal became encased in a box, the skull, for protection. The basic fish shape, with a backbone, fins, and skull, had evolved by Devonian times.

For most of the Earth's history the atmosphere—the air around it—had been a mixture of poisonous gases. Along with the first primitive animals in the sea, the first primitive plants evolved. Plants live by using sunlight as energy to make their food. They give off oxygen as a product of this. While life existed only in the sea, oxygen had been bubbling up from the seaweed and other primitive plants. Eventually, by the Silurian Period, there was enough oxygen in the atmosphere to support life out of the water.

Silurian Period 439–409 million years ago
Common fossils of the Silurian Period include trilobites and corals. Fossils of the first land-living creatures of this time are rare.

Devonian Period 409–363 million years ago
By Devonian times, land life was doing well, but in the sea fish had become very common. The Devonian Period is called the Age of Fish.

BEFORE DINOSAURS

The first vertebrate to live on land was most likely a kind of fish, like the lungfish today. It would have had a lung, so it could breathe air as we do, and paired muscular fins, so it could pull itself over land. It would have been able to live on land for only short periods. This may have allowed it to survive when ponds dried out in dry seasons, or to hunt the insects and spiders that were already living on land.

In Devonian times the first amphibians evolved. These were much like the lungfish. They still had a head and tail like those of a fish. But they also had strong ribs to work the lungs, and proper legs with toes. Some could live out of the water for long periods, yet still had to return to the water to lay eggs.

The Carboniferous Period was a time of rivers with broad deltas and swamps, ideal places for amphibians. All kinds evolved. But the first reptiles developed at this time as well.

Westlothiana

Carboniferous Period 363 million years ago
The Carboniferous coal forests were filled with amphibians and insects, and were also home to the first reptile, *Westlothiana*, shown here.

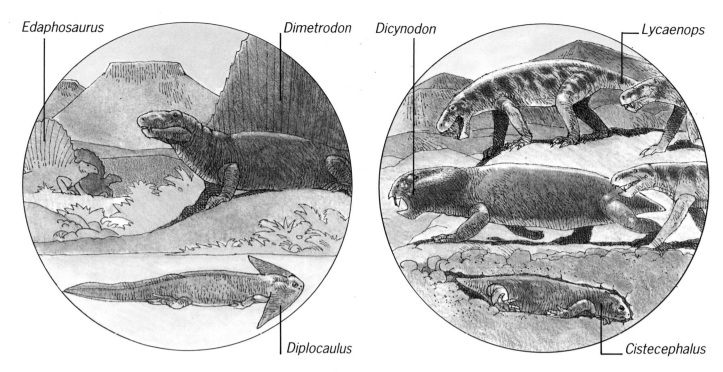

Edaphosaurus · Dimetrodon · Dicynodon · Lycaenops · Diplocaulus · Cistecephalus

Permian Period 290 million years ago
Amphibians flourished in the oases of the Permian deserts, but more successful were reptiles like the herd-living *Edaphosaurus* and *Dimetrodon*, a hunter.

△ The later Permian reptiles were somewhat similar to mammals in their stance, teeth pattern, and appearance, and included rabbitlike *Dicynodon*, wolflike *Lycaenops*, and molelike *Cistecephalus*.

▽ By the Triassic Period, reptiles had developed into many different types. The mammal-like reptiles were still around and included hippopotamus-like *Lystrosaurus*.

The big difference between a reptile and an amphibian is that the reptile lays an egg with a protective covering. Inside, a membrane and fluid allow the developing animal to breathe air. It does not need to live in water.

The following Permian Period was a time of deserts and ice caps. The amphibians adapted to the dry climate by evolving into armored land-living types. It was the reptiles, though, that did best in the drier condition. The main reptile types of that time were mammal-like. They had straight, not sprawling, walking legs, and different-sized teeth like a mammal's.

In the Triassic, the deserts continued. The big amphibians died out. The mammal-like reptiles faded away, but not before the first mammals evolved from them. The thecodonts became most important, evolving into several groups, including the dinosaurs.

21

LATE TRIASSIC PERIOD
245 to 208 million years ago

Conifer

Horsetails

Desmatosuchus

Rutiodon

In the Late Triassic Period, the first phase of the Age of Dinosaurs, the desert conditions still existed over much of our planet. All the continents of the world were jammed together to make up one huge landmass, called Pangaea. This supercontinent was so big that most of it was a long way from the moist winds of the sea, and so hot dry conditions were common. The earlier Permian Period had been a time of mountains, formed as all the separate continents crashed into one another. By the Triassic Period these mountains were mostly worn down to hills.

The animals living in this ancient landscape consisted of the last of the mammal-like reptiles. Among them were *Placerias,* thecodonts such as armored *Desmatosuchus,* and crocodile-like *Rutiodon.* There were also the earliest dinosaurs, for example *Coelophysis.*

Ferns

Placerias

Mountain ranges were still growing up along the edges of the continents. From the young Rocky Mountains, streams tumbled downward and spread rubble and sand over what is now Arizona. Along the routes of these rivers grew groups of conifer trees and cycadeoids, which were plants with swollen trunks that looked like the modern cycads. The small plants covering the ground of these woodlands were mainly ferns. Reed-beds of horsetails lined the riverbanks.

How do we know all this? The remains of all these plants now lie in Petrified Forest National Park in Arizona. The logs of the conifers, turned to stone, lie in the desert landscape where the overlying rock has been worn away by the weather.

In what is now South America, fast-running dinosaurs like _Staurikosaurus_ evolved. In Europe lived _Plateosaurus,_ the first big dinosaur.

△ In an area that is now Arizona grew conifers, cycadeoids, ferns, and giant horsetails. The dinosaur _Coelophysis,_ seen here among the trees, lived alongside crocodile- and mammal-like reptiles.

Coelophysis

23

EARLY AND MIDDLE JURASSIC PERIOD
208 to 157 million years ago

In the early part of the Jurassic Period the supercontinent of Pangaea was still intact. It would not be long, though, before it would begin to split apart. Splits in the land began to form along the line that would tear North America away from Africa.

Shallow seas began to spread across the surface of Pangaea. These brought much more moist climates far inland on the continent, and forests flourished where once there had been deserts. The seas flooded the low land between North America and Africa.

At that time, much of Britain and the continent of Europe consisted of low islands in a shallow sea. Sea reptiles, such as sleek dolphinlike *Ichthyosaurus* and the long-necked *Plesiosaurus,* chased fish and the coil-shelled ammonites in the warm, shallow waters. The islands would have been covered by a plant life looking like that of the Triassic Period. The early armored dinosaur *Scelidosaurus* lived here, and had to guard itself against big meat-eaters, while pterosaurs circled in the sky overhead.

At the other end of Pangaea, where South Africa now lies, there were plant-eating dinosaurs like *Heterodontosaurus* and *Massospondylus,* and meat-eating kinds like *Syntarsus.*

▷ Southern England about 165 million years ago. A *Plesiosaurus* hauls itself up onto the beach, alongside a dead *Ichthyosaurus.* A big meat-eating dinosaur, left, and a *Scelidosaurus*, right, are nearby. *Dimorphodon* fly overhead.

Big meat-eater related to *Megalosaurus*

Dimorphodon

Plesiosaurus

Scelidosaurus

Ichthyosaurus

LATE JURASSIC PERIOD
157 to 146 million years ago

As the Middle Jurassic Period gave way to the Late Jurassic, the supercontinent of Pangaea began slowly to be pulled apart. The shallow seas continued to spread over the low-lying areas. One particular sea, now called the Sundance Sea, spread southward over the continent of North America. It cut off the new Rocky Mountains to the west from the main part of the continent to the east. Sand and pebbles spread out into the sea from the foot of the mountains and formed a broad river plain. In spite of the nearby sea, this plain was quite dry.

Comodactylus

▽ Plant-eating dinosaurs, meat-eating dinosaurs, and pterosaurs lived in and around a coniferous forest on a dry plain in Colorado.

Allosaurus

Stegosaurus

Ornitholestes

Apatosaurus

Brachiosaurus

Ceratosaurus

Mesadactylus

Plants grew in large numbers only along the courses of the many streams. The rocks formed here consist of sandstones, mudstones, and siltstones in a great sequence of layers called the Morrison Formation. Parts of the edges of the layers can be seen in Montana, Utah, Colorado, and New Mexico.

The Morrison Formation is so rich in dinosaur remains that it was the site of great dinosaur hunts in the years between 1877 and 1900. The fossils discovered allow us to imagine the open plain, with forests of conifers and ferns along the waterways, inhabited by big plant-eating dinosaurs like *Apatosaurus* and *Brachiosaurus,* and armored dinosaurs like *Stegosaurus*. These were hunted and killed by meat-eaters like *Ceratosaurus* and *Allosaurus*. Smaller meat-eaters and pterosaurs were there, too.

EARLY CRETACEOUS PERIOD
146 to 97 million years ago

In Early Cretaceous times the split-up of Pangaea was well underway. An ocean had opened up between North America and Africa, although North America and Europe were still joined in the north. Africa and South America were still one landmass, but Antarctica and India had broken away as islands. At the beginning the shallow seas covering northern Europe had gone. A large freshwater lake, the Wealden, was left over southern England and northern France. Around it were ridges of limestone rock formed in the Carboniferous Period, and to the north lay an even older mountain range.

▽ Herds of *Iguanodon* and of *Hypsilophodon* move through the rich vegetation of what is now southeast England.

Iguanodon

Hylaeosaurus

Ornithodesmus

Baryonyx

Hypsilophodon

The dinosaurs that lived around the Wealden lake included *Iguanodon*. It seems to have lived in herds, feeding on horsetail plants. We sometimes find *Iguanodon* footprints in the mudstone, along with skin marks showing where these dinosaurs wallowed in the mud. Living there also were swift-footed *Hypsilophodon*, meat-eating or fish-eating *Baryonyx*, and armored *Hylaeosaurus*. Big pterosaurs, such as *Ornithodesmus*, flew overhead, and early mammals scampered in the ferny undergrowth.

The muds and clays laid down in the Wealden lake are known as the Wealden Formation. They contain fossils of conifer trees, ferns, tree ferns, ginkgoes, and early flowering plants, as well as the animals of the time. Mud cracks and rain pits in the mudstones show where the shallow waters dried out from time to time.

29

LATE CRETACEOUS PERIOD
97 to 65 million years ago

By the Late Cretaceous Period, the end of the Age of Dinosaurs, Pangaea had ceased to exist; the supercontinent had completely broken up. North America was separate from South America and from Europe, and Africa had broken away from South America. However, Antarctica and Australia were still joined, and western North America was connected to northeastern Asia by a land bridge. Many places were covered by shallow seas. A broad shallow sea, the Niobrara Sea, cut North America completely in two from north to south.

▽ Heavily wooded landscape in what is now Wyoming. Herds of *Edmontosaurus* move across country, keeping well clear of *Tyrannosaurus*. Modern-looking birds fly overhead.

Edmontosaurus

Ankylosaurus

Triceratops

Thescelosaurus

Tyrannosaurus

Plant life was changing everywhere. The huge
forests of conifer trees and ferns were being
replaced by modern-looking forests of oak
and willow. Flowering plants formed the
undergrowth. Palm trees grew in the warmer
areas. The region that today is Wyoming had
such a forest, browsed by herds of two-footed
plant-eaters like huge *Edmontosaurus,*
horned dinosaurs like *Triceratops* and
Leptoceratops, and armored giants like
Ankylosaurus. These were all preyed upon by
the great meat-eater *Tyrannosaurus.* The
remains of these dinosaurs have been found in
the rock layers of the Lance Formation.

Leptoceratops

THE RISE OF MAMMALS

The dinosaurs and many other creatures died out suddenly about 65 million years ago, a time that marks the end of the Cretaceous Period. We do not know why this happened. Possibly the moving continents changed the climates too much; the weather became too hot or cold. Maybe diseases spread through the whole dinosaur kingdom. Or perhaps these animals could not cope with the changing plant life. Another possibility is that there was some kind of great disaster. Perhaps the Earth was struck by a giant meteorite. Whatever occurred, the dinosaurs all perished, along with the other great reptiles of the time.

After all the big reptiles were wiped out, the little mammals that had played such a minor part for the previous 160 million years suddenly became important.

The pterosaurs, the flying reptiles, were replaced by winged mammals, the bats. The ichthyosaurs were eventually replaced by swimming mammals, the whales. The different types of dinosaurs—the meat-eaters and the plant-eaters big and small—were replaced by all kinds of meat- and plant-eating mammals. These spread from tropical forests, through deserts to the polar wilderness. The birds, too, spread out and became much more important than they were before.

At first most mammals were forest-living types, but soon the forests gave way to grassy plains. Plains-living mammals later evolved, with long running legs and strong grass-eating teeth. These were the ancestors of the horses and the antelopes. It was the Age of Mammals in which we are living now.

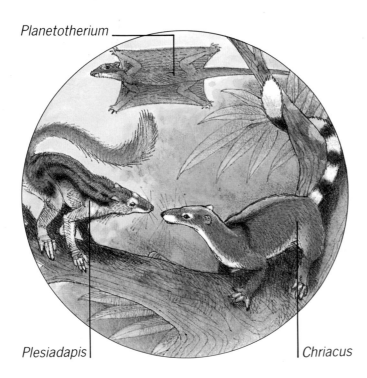

Planetotherium

Plesiadapis

Chriacus

Paleocene times 65 to 56.5 million years ago
The Paleocene forests were home to tree-living mammals like climbing *Plesiadapis* and *Chriacus*, and gliding *Planetotherium*.

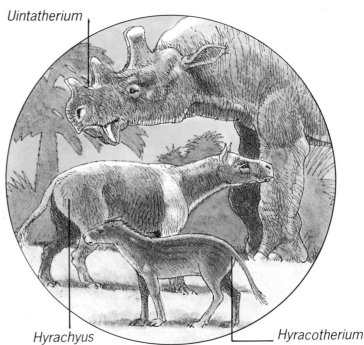

Uintatherium

Hyrachyus

Hyracotherium

Eocene times 56.5 to 35.5 million years ago
In the Eocene forests lived huge rhinoceros-like *Uintatherium*, the little rhinoceros *Hyrachyus*, and the tiny earliest horse *Hyracotherium*.

The Age of Humans

The dinosaurs dominated the Earth for long ages. Today human beings do. All the known history of human beings is measured in thousands of years. The emergence of human beings—unique, self-conscious creatures—is a mystery. Scientists are tracking down physical clues like the similarity of other "hominids" (shown here) and man. There is much still to be learned; you may help learn it.

Brontotherium

Hyaenodon

Archaeotherium

Hoplophoneus

Megatylopus

Pliohippus

Epigaulus

Amebelodon

Synthetoceras

Oligocene times 35.5 to 23.5 million years ago
The open landscapes of the Oligocene Epoch had big plant-eaters, *Brontotherium* and *Archaeotherium*, and meat-eating *Hyaenodon* and *Hoplophoneus*.

Miocene times 23.5 to 5.2 million years ago
The Miocene grasslands had the horse *Pliohippus*, gazellelike *Synthetoceras*, the camel *Megatylopus*, the rodent *Epigaulus*, and the elephant *Amebelodon*.

Within the fact panel for each dinosaur we show a way of pronouncing the animal's name easily, and have listed the animal's most important features and where its remains have been found. A black oval on the little bar chart shows through which geological periods the animal lived. On the chart, mya is an abbreviation of *millions of years ago*. The drawing of the dinosaur is labelled to show the main body features. A scale diagram compares the size of the dinosaur to a 6-foot-tall person.

The Age of Dinosaurs

The first dinosaurs appeared about 225 million years ago (mya for short) in what scientists call the Late Triassic Period. They thrived through the following Jurassic Period and died out at the end of the Cretaceous Period 65 million years ago. During this time, geography, climate, and vegetation, or plant life, were constantly changing—as shown in these dinosaur scenes.

Triassic 245–208 mya
A single giant landmass or supercontinent, mostly desert conditions, tree ferns, and conifers.

Early and Middle Jurassic 208–157 mya Supercontinent, shallow seas, moist climate, tree ferns, conifers, and cycads.

TWO

The Real Monsters

The dinosaurs were the giants of the Earth. They existed for about 160 million years, and during this time some of them developed into the biggest and most powerful animals that the Earth has seen. The plant-eaters were the biggest. Their enormous bodies contained digestive systems that could break down tons of vegetable material and use it as fuel to keep them alive. Massive meat-eating dinosaurs evolved as well, frequently hunting down and feeding on these moving mountains of meat. As a defense against the vicious claws and the tearing teeth, several groups of big plant-eating dinosaurs developed tough armor and weapons. Shields and horns evolved, making the plant-eaters heavier still.

All these prehistoric giants are not just interesting in their own right. Their remains, which we call fossils, can tell us about what the world was like in past times—how the climates have changed, how the continents have moved, and so on. And as we try to build up a picture of what dinosaurs looked like and how they all lived, we realize some of the wonders of nature. The structure of large dinosaurs has been a bit of a mystery: How did they eat enough to keep the huge bodies fueled? How could such a heavy animal be supported on only four legs? Now we are finding that the techniques which engineers have invented to build bridges and cranes were developed by nature millions of years ago. They appeared during the evolution of the different types of skeleton structures of the giant dinosaurs, the greatest animals that ever walked the Earth.

Late Jurassic 157–146 mya
Supercontinent beginning to break up, dry inland, moist climates by coasts.

Early Cretaceous 146–97 mya
Continents drifting into separate landmasses, plant life as in Triassic and Jurassic periods.

Late Cretaceous 97–65 mya
Separate continents, each with its own animal life, and plants like modern types.

PLATEOSAURUS—stretching out to eat

Imagine the big land animals of today—elephants, giraffes, rhinoceroses, buffalos. What one thing do they all have in common? The answer is that they all eat plants. Modern meat-eaters, such as lions, wolves, and foxes, are all much smaller. One major reason for this is that vast amounts of plant material must be digested to gain enough nutrients. So a plant-eater's guts—its stomach and intestines—must be much larger than a meat-eater's to do the work.

It was the same in the dinosaur world. The first dinosaurs, in Late Triassic times, were small, fast-moving meat-eaters, running about on their hind legs. Then the plant-eating dinosaurs evolved. Their big intestines meant that they had a long body and could not balance on their hind legs anymore. They began to move about on all fours.

The early plant-eating dinosaurs could still rear up on their hind legs for short periods, and this was a good thing for them. There were other plant-eating reptiles about, but they were like lizards and could only eat the fern and horsetail plants growing near the ground. The first plant-eating dinosaurs were the only animals that could reach up and eat the leaves and conifer needles from the tops of the trees. They developed long necks as well, and this helped them to reach up still farther.

Living in large groups

Plateosaurus was typical of these early plant-eating dinosaurs. There must have been many of them as several skeletons of *Plateosaurus* have been found together in one Late Triassic deposit in Germany. Some scientists think that this is because the animal lived and moved about in herds, but others are not so sure. Maybe dead *Plateosaurus* from a wide area were washed into a hollow in the ground when the desert streams flooded. The oases, or water holes, of the desert landscape probably had enough trees growing around them to support many thousands of these dinosaurs.

▽ *Plateosaurus* feeds among tree ferns on a hot, dusty Late Triassic plain. The arms of *Plateosaurus* were strong to support the front part of the animal on the ground. It could move its hands about freely. It used its thumb claws to pull down vegetation or to fight off enemies.

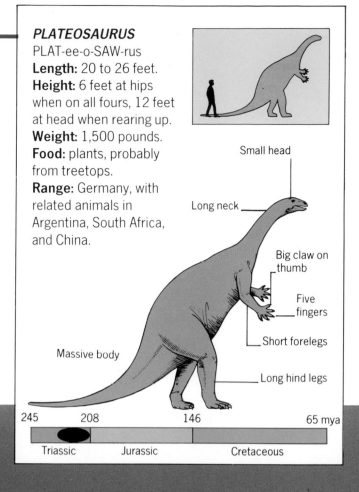

PLATEOSAURUS
PLAT-ee-o-SAW-rus
Length: 20 to 26 feet.
Height: 6 feet at hips when on all fours, 12 feet at head when rearing up.
Weight: 1,500 pounds.
Food: plants, probably from treetops.
Range: Germany, with related animals in Argentina, South Africa, and China.

Small head

Long neck

Big claw on thumb

Five fingers

Short forelegs

Long hind legs

Massive body

245	208	146	65 mya
Triassic	Jurassic	Cretaceous	

DILOPHOSAURUS—crests and sharp teeth

The big plant-eating dinosaurs such as *Plateosaurus* evolved at the end of the Triassic Period. Big meat-eaters evolved as well and, by the beginning of the Jurassic, there were many different types. *Dilophosaurus* was one of these. Whenever there is a new type of food available, something will evolve to eat it. A big plant-eating animal has lots of flesh, so big meat-eating animals evolve to hunt them. *Dilophosaurus* was one of the first big meat-eating dinosaurs, yet it looked like one of the small meat-eaters, with a slim and athletic body. Its jaws were armed with long sharp teeth that it used for tearing up chunks of meat—possibly the bodies of all kinds of *Plateosaurus*-like dinosaurs.

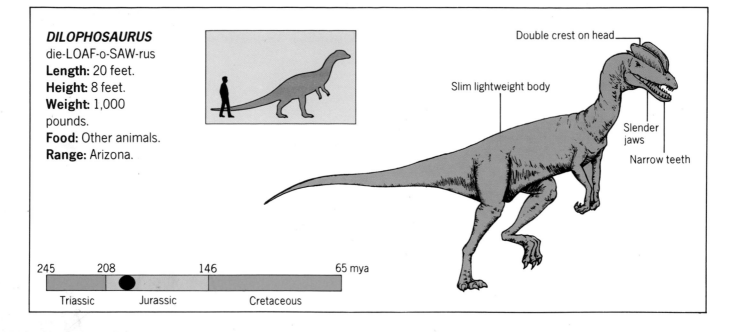

DILOPHOSAURUS
die-LOAF-o-SAW-rus
Length: 20 feet.
Height: 8 feet.
Weight: 1,000 pounds.
Food: Other animals.
Range: Arizona.

Double crest on head

Slim lightweight body

Slender jaws

Narrow teeth

245	208	146	65 mya
Triassic	Jurassic	Cretaceous	

A name meaning "two-ridged reptile"

The front of the snout of this dinosaur was especially narrow and flexible. Maybe *Dilophosaurus* hunted small prey, too, pulling out lizards and small mammals from the undergrowth and crannies in rocks.

Its skull is different from that of the later big meat-eaters. Not only did *Dilophosaurus* have the bone joints that allowed it to wrinkle its nose, but it also had a pair of bony crests along the top of its head—hence its name. However, as in most dinosaurs, the skull is the most fragile part of the skeleton. It was missing from the first skeleton of *Dilophosaurus* to be found. The scientists who found the skeleton did not realize just what a strange animal they had discovered.

◁ Prowling by the coniferous forests of Early Jurassic Arizona, crested *Dilophosaurus* surprises a small *Syntarsus*, another crested meat-eating dinosaur. The crests of these animals were probably brightly colored and would have been used for signaling.

39

STEGOSAURUS—all plates and spikes

Imagine an animal about the size of an elephant, with short front legs. Instead of an elephant's big head and trunk, give it a little head no longer than your forearm, with narrow jaws and a beak. Give it a tail as long as its body. Now stand a double row of triangular plates along the back. These range from the size of a saucer on the neck and tail to the size of a truck wheel in the middle of the animal above its hips. Put a bunch of vicious-looking spines on the tail's tip.

You have imagined *Stegosaurus*.

This was a plant-eater that lived in North America in Late Jurassic times. It used its narrow beak to probe among the prickly leaves of cycadlike plants known as cycadeoids and to nip out the tasty shoots.

The plates on its back may have been covered with skin. In the hot dry open landscape where *Stegosaurus* lived, the wind blowing around the plates would have kept the animal cool.

▷ Dust blows across a plain in Late Jurassic Colorado. A *Stegosaurus* turns its body into the wind to cool itself. Few creatures posed a threat to the big plant-eater. There were huge hunting dinosaurs about, and it must have defended itself against them with its spiked tail.

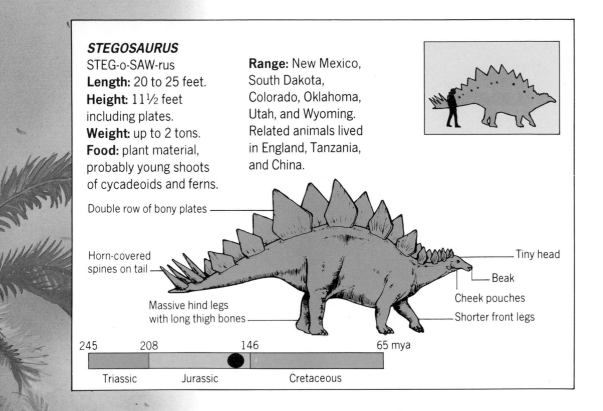

STEGOSAURUS
STEG-o-SAW-rus
Length: 20 to 25 feet.
Height: 11½ feet including plates.
Weight: up to 2 tons.
Food: plant material, probably young shoots of cycadeoids and ferns.

Range: New Mexico, South Dakota, Colorado, Oklahoma, Utah, and Wyoming. Related animals lived in England, Tanzania, and China.

Double row of bony plates

Horn-covered spines on tail

Tiny head

Beak

Cheek pouches

Massive hind legs with long thigh bones

Shorter front legs

245	208	146	65 mya
Triassic	Jurassic	Cretaceous	

Defense or display?

On the other hand, the plates may have been covered with horn and used as a defense against fierce meat-eating dinosaurs. We are still not sure what the plates did. Certainly the spikes on the tail were weapons, and the tail could be swung with a terrible force at an attacking meat-eater.

We are also unclear how the plates of *Stegosaurus* were actually arranged—in pairs, staggered in two rows, or a single row overlapping. They may well have been brightly colored to act as signals to other dinosaurs, perhaps to attract mates.

Stegosaurus fossils are found in layers of rock that lie at the foot of the Rocky Mountains from New Mexico to South Dakota. There were at least two species of *Stegosaurus*. One had small plates and four pairs of tail spines. The other had larger plates and two pairs of tail spines.

41

APATOSAURUS—eating leaves and pebbles

Across the dry plains of the North American landscape comes a herd of huge animals, their shapes unclear in the clouds of dust kicked up. Long necks with tiny heads sway about as the mass lumbers slowly onwards—a moving mountain of flesh and dust. This is the Late Jurassic Period, the time of the largest dinosaurs. The animals are *Apatosaurus,* among the biggest land animals that ever lived.

A group of coniferous trees grows by the riverbank, shading a clump of ferns and cycadlike plants. The *Apatosaurus* herd moves from the sun-baked plains in among the trees, the dust settles, and the great beasts begin to feed.

The huge body of an *Apatosaurus* needed constant feeding. The animal must have spent most of its time eating. The skeleton of the long neck was extremely light, made of narrow strips and sheets of bone. These supported the neck just as steel beams and sheets hold up a bridge. The tiny head could

42

swing about allowing *Apatosaurus* to feed on the low vegetation or stretch up to eat from the tops of the trees. The hips of this dinosaur were very heavy, and the hip muscles were strong enough to allow it to rear up on its hind legs for short periods.

The teeth of *Apatosaurus* were narrow and peglike, and arranged like a comb along the jaws. They raked the fronds off the fern plants and the leaves from the twigs of the high trees. There was no time for chewing. The food was just swallowed as quickly as it was plucked. Down the long throat it went until it reached the digestive system. There it may have been ground down by means of pebbles that *Apatosaurus* swallowed from time to time for just this job.

Scientists think this is possible because they have found heaps of rounded pebbles in the stomach areas of *Apatosaurus* skeletons. Many birds use stones in this way, since they cannot chew with their toothless beaks.

▽ A big bull *Apatosaurus* leads his family herd through the Late Jurassic woodlands. As in an elephant, the animal's massive legs supported its great weight. The feet had thick pads of gristle behind the toes that acted as cushion soles. The tail was long and narrow, and could have been used as a whip to strike at attacking meat-eaters.

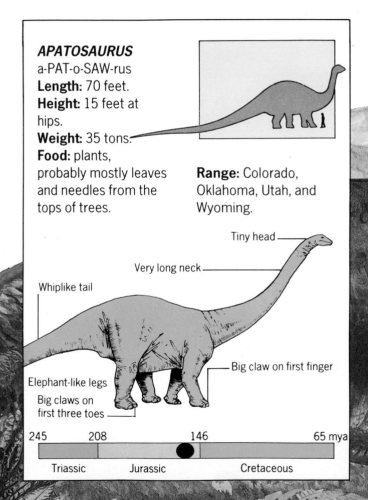

APATOSAURUS
a-PAT-o-SAW-rus
Length: 70 feet.
Height: 15 feet at hips.
Weight: 35 tons.
Food: plants, probably mostly leaves and needles from the tops of trees.

Range: Colorado, Oklahoma, Utah, and Wyoming.

Tiny head

Very long neck

Whiplike tail

Big claw on first finger

Elephant-like legs

Big claws on first three toes

245	208	146	65 mya
Triassic	Jurassic		Cretaceous

BRACHIOSAURUS—long neck, small head

In 1900, parts of the skeleton of one of these massive dinosaurs were found in Colorado, in the same rock formation that contained the remains of *Stegosaurus, Apatosaurus, Allosaurus,* and many of the other huge Jurassic dinosaurs.

Then, seven years later, the complete skeleton of the same animal was discovered in Tanzania—half the world away. It also was found along with skeletons of relatives of *Stegosaurus* and *Allosaurus.* Obviously the same kinds of animals lived in similar environments in widely separated places on Earth. In Late Jurassic times all the continents were still joined together in one big landmass, and many animals had the freedom to wander all over it.

Brachiosaurus was a truly enormous animal, and like *Apatosaurus* was one that was able to browse in the highest trees. But unlike *Apatosaurus* it did not have the muscles to allow it to rear up on its hind legs. Instead it had very long front legs that gave it high

shoulders. From this high platform the neck could reach up into the branches to browse the twigs and leaves that would have been out of the reach of other plant-eaters. The top half of the animal was lightweight, with its skull and backbones made of thin strips and sheets of bone. The leg bones and ribs, however, were thick and massive. This whole structure produced a stable base from which *Brachiosaurus* could reach around for food.

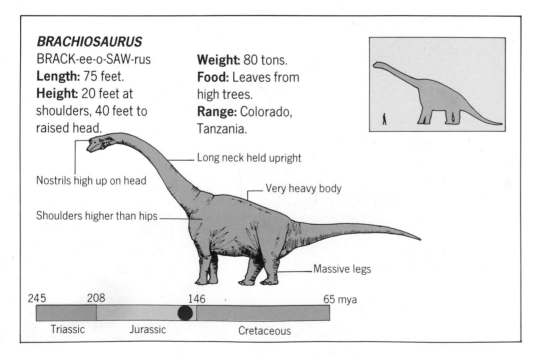

BRACHIOSAURUS
BRACK-ee-o-SAW-rus
Length: 75 feet.
Height: 20 feet at shoulders, 40 feet to raised head.
Weight: 80 tons.
Food: Leaves from high trees.
Range: Colorado, Tanzania.

Nostrils high up on head
Shoulders higher than hips
Long neck held upright
Very heavy body
Massive legs

245	208	146	65 mya
Triassic	Jurassic	Cretaceous	

△ A close modern-day equivalent of *Brachiosaurus* is the giraffe. It too has high shoulders and an elongated neck that can reach up to the twigs of the highest branches.

▷ Held 40 feet above the ground, the tiny head of *Brachiosaurus* had nostrils that were huge. They were probably lined with moist skin that helped to keep the great body cool in the hot, dry environments.

ALLOSAURUS—moving in packs

A 3-foot-long head, with jaws open wide and armed with sawlike teeth, bites into the thigh of a young *Camptosaurus,* ripping back the skin, tearing away flesh, and scraping along the bone. Making no more than a panicking hiss sound, for its tiny brain cannot sense pain, the unfortunate animal collapses on its belly in the dust. Its attacker, an adult *Allosaurus,* releases the leg and lunges for the animal's throat.

Allosaurus uses the huge claw on its first finger to hook into the skin of its victim's neck. With its great mouth it bites down once more to finish the kill. The rest of the stampeding *Camptosaurus* herd slow down;

their first rush of panic is over. They forget their companion—it is lost to the herd. They forget the *Allosaurus* as well since it poses no danger now that it has made its kill. The remainder of the *Allosaurus* pack gather round to feast. Smaller dinosaurs, such as *Ornitholestes,* approach later, looking for an opportunity to dart in and steal a piece of meat. Perhaps pterosaurs circle above, ready to scavenge anything left over.

All this, of course, is what we think may have happened. However, we do know that the big plant-eaters of Late Jurassic North America were preyed upon by the huge meat-eater *Allosaurus.*

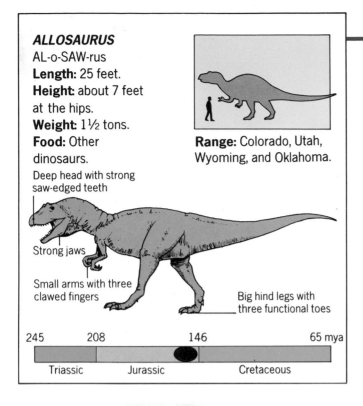

ALLOSAURUS

AL-o-SAW-rus

Length: 25 feet.

Height: about 7 feet at the hips.

Weight: 1½ tons.

Food: Other dinosaurs.

Range: Colorado, Utah, Wyoming, and Oklahoma.

Deep head with strong saw-edged teeth

Strong jaws

Small arms with three clawed fingers

Big hind legs with three functional toes

245	208	146	65 mya
Triassic	Jurassic	Cretaceous	

In the rocks of the time are skeletons that have been torn apart with great ferocity, with deep grooves in the bones scored by *Allosaurus* teeth, and with broken *Allosaurus* teeth scattered around.

Allosaurus was the biggest and strongest meat-eater of the time. It could move swiftly on its powerful hind legs, its head with the great killing teeth held forward, balanced by the long stiff tail. The front legs were small, but each had three powerful claws.

◁ Using its huge teeth, the enormous *Allosaurus* rips into the body of a *Camptosaurus*, an American relative of *Iguanodon*. The teeth had sawlike rear edges. They worked like steak knives, the muscles of the skull moving the upper and lower jaws back and forth, tearing the food between them. The skull and jaws could bulge outward to gulp huge chunks of meat.

IGUANODON—thumbs-up

Iguanodon was typical of the big plant-eating dinosaurs that took over from the long-necked herbivores in Early Cretaceous times. Instead of plucking and swallowing huge masses of plant materials that were then ground up by stones in the stomach, these animals were able to chew their plant food thoroughly before swallowing it. A horny beak at the front of the jaws allowed them to gather food, and strong banks of grinding teeth could shred and pulp it as it was churned about in large cheek pouches.

Herds of *Iguanodon* roamed the swampy shores of a vast lake that lay over much of northern Europe at that time. We can see footprints of the herds in the rocks. Now and again they wallowed in the mud of the reed-beds of horsetails on which they grazed. We have found their skin prints in the same rocks.

From two-footed to all fours

There were big meat-eaters around, too, probably on the hunt for young or weak *Iguanodon*. Skeletons of young *Iguanodon* have short front legs compared with the adults'. It seems likely that the youngsters moved about mostly on their hind legs and could defend themselves by running away from their enemies. The adults were slower, going around mostly on all fours. They had large plates of bone in the chest area that helped the front legs support the heavier body. The adults' sheer size would protect them from most attackers.

▷ *Iguanodon* browse in the thickets, sometimes walking on all fours, sometimes rising on their hind legs to pull down leafy boughs. Their hands, with three strong middle fingers, a thumb spike, and a flexible fifth finger, could be used for both walking and collecting food.

IGUANODON
ig-WA-no-don

Length: 33 feet.
Height: 15 feet to head when on hind legs.
Weight: Up to 6 tons.
Food: Plants, particularly horsetails, ferns, and cycads.

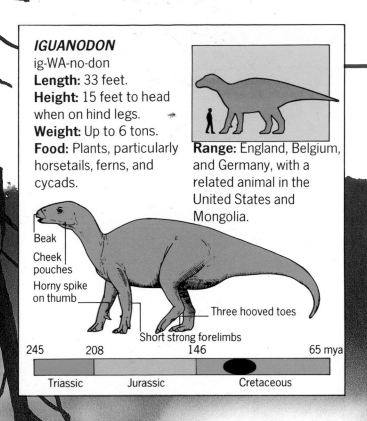

Range: England, Belgium, and Germany, with a related animal in the United States and Mongolia.

Beak
Cheek pouches
Horny spike on thumb
Three hooved toes
Short strong forelimbs

245	208	146	65 mya
Triassic	Jurassic	Cretaceous	

▷ Like *Iguanodon*, the modern okapi grazes vegetation in warm, moist forests. *Iguanodon* may have had a tongue like the okapi's, which is about 16 inches long, for pulling off leaves and twigs to eat.

BARYONYX—big fish-eater

Although most dinosaurs fit into a few basic recognizable shapes, once in a while we discover one that is quite different. *Baryonyx* is one of these.

It was one of the large meat-eating dinosaurs, with a low-slung body balanced at the strong hind legs by a long tail. However, the neck was held quite straight, not in an S-shape as in other meat-eating dinosaurs. The jaws were long and narrow and full of tiny pointed teeth, giving the head the appearance of a crocodile. The front legs were very large, and the first finger, the thumb, carried a huge claw more than 12 inches long. The name *Baryonyx* means "heavy claw."

What could such a creature have eaten?
Some bits and pieces of the last meal were found in the stomach area of the only skeleton of *Baryonyx* to have been discovered. These were mostly the scales and bones of fish. So clearly *Baryonyx* was a fish-eater—the only fish-eating dinosaur known.

We can now imagine the dinosaur crouched patiently on the banks of an Early Cretaceous stream that flowed into the great North European lake, awaiting its prey. With a sudden lunge and a splash of water, it hooks out a large fish with its great claw and snaps it up in its mouth as the fish thrashes about on the stream bank.

▷ In the modern world, grizzly bears gather on riverbanks when the salmon are migrating. They use their teeth or claws to catch the fish. Possibly *Baryonyx* hunted in a similar way.

◁ *Baryonyx* fishes in an Early Cretaceous shallow lake in southern England. It uses its crocodile-like jaws with 32 teeth on each side to catch prey.

Baryonyx uses the many small teeth in its long jaws to hold the slippery prey firmly, then carries the fish off into the ferny shade of the conifer trees to eat.

Scientists also found bits of *Iguanodon* bone lying in the *Baryonyx* stomach cavity. We cannot really visualize this dinosaur attacking something like an *Iguanodon*. *Baryonyx* could possibly have used its big claws for killing, but its teeth are not the correct shape or size for that kind of hunting.

Perhaps *Baryonyx* was a scavenger as well as a fisher, using its long jaws to reach inside dead dinosaurs to reach the soft innards, just as vultures do today.

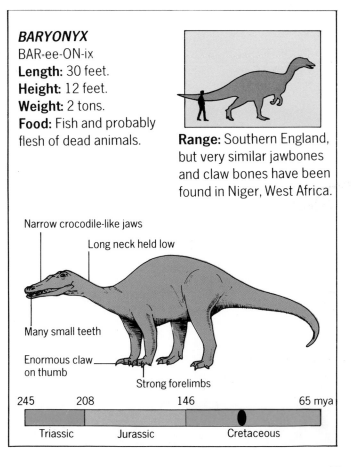

BARYONYX
BAR-ee-ON-ix
Length: 30 feet.
Height: 12 feet.
Weight: 2 tons.
Food: Fish and probably flesh of dead animals.

Range: Southern England, but very similar jawbones and claw bones have been found in Niger, West Africa.

Narrow crocodile-like jaws

Long neck held low

Many small teeth

Enormous claw on thumb

Strong forelimbs

245	208	146	65 mya
Triassic	Jurassic	Cretaceous	

SPINOSAURUS—a sail on its back

Here is a mystery. An enormous meat-eating dinosaur, among the biggest that ever lived, with a huge sail down its back, and a narrow, crocodile-like head. What do we make of this?

The sail was supported by a series of long spines, each growing straight up from a backbone. Some of these spines were as tall as a person. A sail on the back is not an unusual feature. In modern animals we find it in basilisk lizards and water dragons, where it is used for display, for signaling to mates. *Spinosaurus* may have used its sail for the same job. If so, the sail would have been brightly colored so it could be seen from afar.

Clues but no evidence

In Permian times, before the dinosaurs evolved, there were sail-backed amphibians and mammal-like reptiles. They lived in hot dry places. The sails were probably used to control the animals' temperatures. When the animals became too hot, they held the sails to the wind to cool the blood. When it was cold, they held the sails to the Sun to warm themselves. This may also have been the purpose of the *Spinosaurus* sail.

Its crocodile-like head and small teeth were like those of *Baryonyx*. This suggests that *Spinosaurus*, too, was a fish-eater. However, a cooling sail would only have been useful in a hot dry landscape, where fish would have been rare!

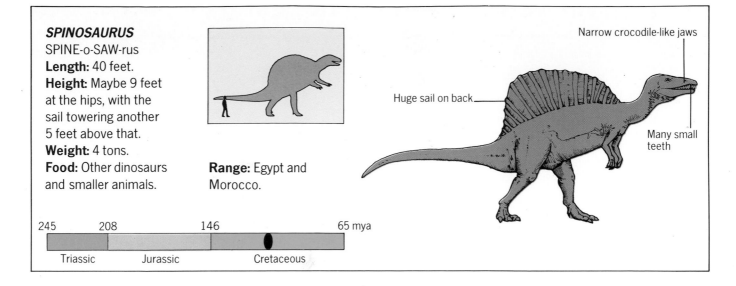

SPINOSAURUS
SPINE-o-SAW-rus
Length: 40 feet.
Height: Maybe 9 feet
at the hips, with the
sail towering another
5 feet above that.
Weight: 4 tons.
Food: Other dinosaurs
and smaller animals.

Range: Egypt and
Morocco.

Narrow crocodile-like jaws

Huge sail on back

Many small
teeth

245	208	146	65 mya
Triassic	Jurassic	Cretaceous	

Anyhow, it is unlikely that such a huge animal could have survived on a diet consisting entirely of fish.

It is extremely difficult for scientists to make up their minds about problems like this, especially since the best remains of *Spinosaurus* were destroyed when the German museum that stored them was bombed during World War II.

◁ Ignoring the flesh of a small plant-eater, a *Spinosaurus* slinks off to rest in the shade of the sparse vegetation of North Africa. *Spinosaurus* must have been the terror of the animal life of the time. Although the best specimen of *Spinosaurus* was destroyed, odd fragments were discovered in the Sahara Desert in the 1980s.

SALTASAURUS—long neck and armored back

▽ *Saltasaurus* pushes its way through the Late Cretaceous vegetation, its broad back presenting a shield of solid armor to any attacker. It could rear up on its hind legs like *Apatosaurus*. It probably had a head shaped like that of *Apatosaurus*, too.

By the end of the Cretaceous Period most of the long-necked leaf-eating dinosaurs had died out. Their places had been taken by animals like *Iguanodon*, which ate ferns and chunks of trees with their beaks and grinding teeth. However, in some places the leaf-eaters lived on. South America was one such place. At the end of the Cretaceous, it was an island continent, and it was inhabited by animals that lived nowhere else. This is rather like Australia today with its kangaroos, echidnas, and koalas. The beaked dinosaurs did not do especially well in South America and the long-necked plant-eaters thrived.

Saltasaurus was one of these. The amazing thing about it was that it was armored. There were many types of armored dinosaurs, but no one thought that the long-necked tree-eaters could carry armor plates. Until the discovery of *Saltasaurus* in the late 1970s, it was thought that they could defend themselves by their sheer size and using their whiplike tails.

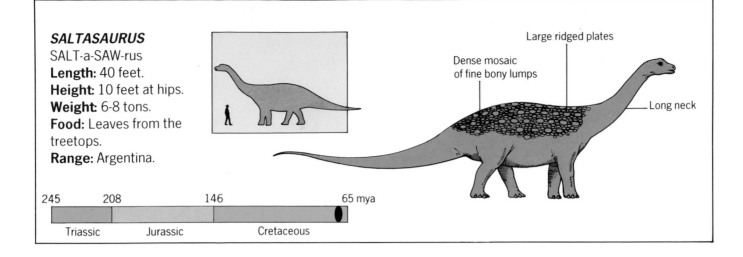

SALTASAURUS
SALT-a-SAW-rus
Length: 40 feet.
Height: 10 feet at hips.
Weight: 6-8 tons.
Food: Leaves from the treetops.
Range: Argentina.

Dense mosaic of fine bony lumps
Large ridged plates
Long neck

245	208	146	65 mya
Triassic	Jurassic	Cretaceous	

Now, *Saltasaurus* was a tree-eater that was big, had a long tail, but was covered in armor, too. The armor consisted of a mosaic, or jigsaw-puzzlelike pattern, of bony buttons, each about half the size of your thumbnail, and a number of saucer-sized plates that may have been the bases of pointed spines.

The Late Cretaceous was a time of very large meat-eating dinosaurs, and South America had its share of them. Body armor like this would have been a useful defense.

55

EUOPLOCEPHALUS—like a tank

The armored dinosaurs called the ankylosaurs were the most heavily armored of all types. They became widespread in the Cretaceous Period, and there were many different types towards the end of their era. *Euoplocephalus* was a typical member of the whole group.

The armor began at the head. The skull was a rigid box of bone, in which even the eyelids were armored bony shutters. *Euoplocephalus* means "well-armored head." Over the neck were broad bony plates, and farther back the shoulders were protected by cone-shaped spines. In life, these plates and spines were probably covered by horn. The broad back was protected by a mosaic of bony studs and bands of circular plates.

The tail was stiff and straight, the bones lashed together by tendons to make a rigid rod. At the end of the tail was a heavy bony club. This tail club was *Euoplocephalus*'s weapon. When a big meat-eater attacked, *Euoplocephalus* could swing its club with a devastating force against the legs of the attacker. (There were meat-eaters like *Albertosaurus,* a relative of *Tyrannosaurus,* in the area.) Although most of the tail was stiff, the joints at the tail's base were very flexible.

Euoplocephalus, and the ankylosaurs in general, had weak teeth. They could not be used for much chewing. It does not seem to have swallowed stones to grind up its food, as the long-necked plant-eaters may have done.

△ Startled by a hungry *Albertosaurus*, the *Euoplocephalus* prepares its defense. Despite the great weight of its armor, *Euoplocephalus* was agile and would have been able to react swiftly when attacked.

Instead it may have had a very complicated stomach for breaking down plant food. Certainly the body was broad and barrel-like, supported by great arches of curving ribs and enormous hip bones, giving plenty of room for a large complex digestive system. *Euoplocephalus* would have used its broad beak to pluck low-growing plants. Then it would have chopped them with its cheek teeth and swallowed the meal to be broken down by lengthy chemical processes.

EUOPLOCEPHALUS
You-oh-plo-SEF-alus
Length: 20 feet.
Height: 5 feet at hips.
Weight: 2-3 tons.
Food: Low-growing plants.
Range: Alberta in Canada.

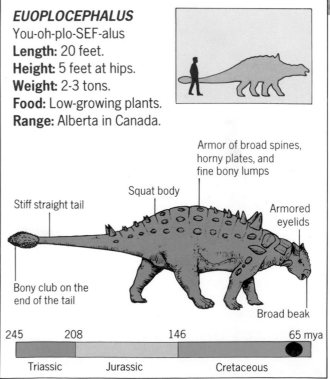

Armor of broad spines, horny plates, and fine bony lumps

Squat body

Stiff straight tail

Armored eyelids

Bony club on the end of the tail

Broad beak

245	208	146	65 mya
Triassic	Jurassic	Cretaceous	

TRICERATOPS—armor and weapons

◁ Like a rhinoceros, *Triceratops* turns to face its attacker, presenting its great horns and its armored frill. *Triceratops* means "three-horned head." Its size and the weapons on its face could keep any natural enemy at bay. All modern rhinoceroses are smaller than *Triceratops* and mostly eat grass—a plant food that had not evolved at *Triceratops*'s time.

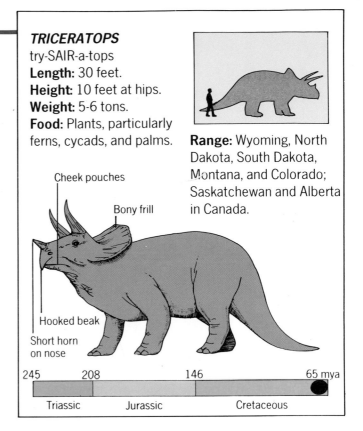

TRICERATOPS
try-SAIR-a-tops
Length: 30 feet.
Height: 10 feet at hips.
Weight: 5-6 tons.
Food: Plants, particularly ferns, cycads, and palms.

Range: Wyoming, North Dakota, South Dakota, Montana, and Colorado; Saskatchewan and Alberta in Canada.

Cheek pouches

Bony frill

Hooked beak

Short horn on nose

245   208   146   65 mya

Triassic   Jurassic   Cretaceous

Three great horns jutting from an armored face. A frill of bone protecting the neck and shoulders. A body the size of an elephant. This is what an attacker would face, should it be unwise enough to attack an adult *Triceratops*.

The ceratopsians—the horn-headed dinosaurs—evolved in the Late Cretaceous Period. They were mostly large animals and all had head horns and a neck frill. Some had just one horn on the nose. Others had two horns over the eyes. A few had all three horns. In some types the frill was short, while in others it was huge and sail-like. Often the frill itself carried horns and spikes. The ceratopsians were the last group of dinosaurs to evolve, and they lived to the very end of the Age of Dinosaurs.

Triceratops was the largest of the ceratopsians. There must have been many *Triceratops* around at the time. Their remains are found all over its range. This dinosaur probably lived in herds, migrating in search of food as seasons changed. Sometimes we come across masses of ceratopsian skeletons together, suggesting that a herd was washed away in a flood while trying to cross a river.

Imagining what must have been
The head of *Triceratops* was a solid mass of armored bone, and so the skull is often well-preserved as a fossil. This is unusual in a dinosaur, because most dinosaur skulls are very lightly built, and easily broken and lost. Impressive though the skull is, it gives only part of the picture of the animal. What seem to be horns are just the bony horn cores. In life these would have been coated with sheaths of true horn, which would have made the structures far longer than they appear on the skeleton. The animal's great beak would also have been covered with horn.

Triceratops probably ate the leaves of the newly evolved palm trees as well as those of the various cycads.

TYRANNOSAURUS—a mighty hunter

Tyrannosaurus, the "tyrant reptile," the biggest and heaviest of all the meat-eating dinosaurs, stalks through the modern-looking forests of oak and magnolia trees. Whiplike willow branches brush along the sides of its body, and the hooves of its three-toed feet sink deep into the leaves covering the forest floor. The trees are thick with leaves in the moist soil close to the water, and the *Tyrannosaurus* is hidden among the shadows. Down by the edge of the lake are several herds of its prey. One of these is a group of *Edmontosaurus*—dinosaurs like *Iguanodon* but with a flattened ducklike bill. They are searching for food. The *Tyrannosaurus* silently awaits their approach.

Suddenly it charges. Pushing with its massive legs, it thrusts itself forward out of the hiding place. It holds its mouth open so its 6-inch-long teeth stick forward, and it keeps its little arms tucked out of the way against its chest. Its stiff straight tail balances its body. Now the great animal charges. It makes no sound, but the noise of the crashing of the bushes and the undergrowth is frightening enough.

With its little eyes pointing forward, it focuses on the nearest *Edmontosaurus*. Its brain judges the distance accurately and, before the *Edmontosaurus* can move, the great jaws sweep down. *Tyrannosaurus* tears out a strip of flesh several inches deep and about 3 feet long, down the plant-eater's thigh. The *Edmontosaurus* collapses, slowly dying of shock and loss of blood, and the great jaws lunge again. Other members of the *Edmontosaurus* herd scatter in panic, leaving the *Tyrannosaurus* to its feast.

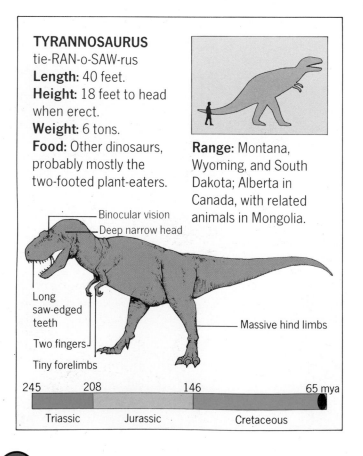

TYRANNOSAURUS
tie-RAN-o-SAW-rus
Length: 40 feet.
Height: 18 feet to head when erect.
Weight: 6 tons.
Food: Other dinosaurs, probably mostly the two-footed plant-eaters.

Range: Montana, Wyoming, and South Dakota; Alberta in Canada, with related animals in Mongolia.

- Binocular vision
- Deep narrow head
- Long saw-edged teeth
- Two fingers
- Tiny forelimbs
- Massive hind limbs

245	208	146	65 mya
Triassic	Jurassic	Cretaceous	

▷ *Tyrannosaurus* hurtles in for the kill, its whole body designed for fast attack. The head and the massively muscled jaws were armed with long teeth that had a sawlike surface along the rear edge. *Tyrannosaurus* probably was the most terrible hunter that ever lived.

Within the fact panel for each dinosaur we show a way of pronouncing the animal's name easily, and have listed the animal's most important features and where its remains have been found. A black oval on the little bar chart shows through which geological periods the animal lived. On the chart, mya is an abbreviation of *millions of years ago*. The drawing of the dinosaur is labelled to show the main body features. A scale diagram compares the size of the dinosaur to a 6-foot-tall person.

The Age of Dinosaurs

The first dinosaurs appeared about 225 million years ago (mya for short) in what scientists call the Late Triassic Period. They thrived through the following Jurassic Period and died out at the end of the Cretaceous Period 65 million years ago. During this time, geography, climate, and vegetation, or plant life, were constantly changing—as shown in these dinosaur scenes.

Triassic 245–208 mya
A single giant landmass or supercontinent, mostly desert conditions, tree ferns, and conifers.

Early and Middle Jurassic 208–157 mya Supercontinent, shallow seas, moist climate, tree ferns, conifers, and cycads.

THREE

All Shapes and Sizes

"Dinosaurs!" Mention the word and what do we think about? Huge five-ton meat-eaters charging through dank forests, their huge claws ready to grab and kill any animal. Gigantic mountains or chunks of living tissue, lumbering slowly across the swamp, each with a tiny head on a long neck reaching for the leaves of tree ferns. Long-legged tree-eaters browsing the topmost branches. Reptilian tanks, coated with armor, bristling with spikes and horns.

What a spectacle! And indeed all these kinds of creatures did exist during the Age of Dinosaurs. Some of the dinosaurs were among the biggest land animals that walked the Earth. However, along with these there lived considerably smaller dinosaurs—little chicken-sized beasts that scuttled about in the undergrowth at the feet of the giants. There were also medium-sized dinosaurs, as big as pigs and sheep. They were all adapted to exist in particular ways in the landscapes of the times. These smaller dinosaurs showed all the dinosaur features to be found among the giants. They also displayed all kinds of other features that enabled them to live in totally different ways—as scavengers, as insect-eaters, as egg-stealers. The animal life of the Age of Dinosaurs was as varied and exciting as is the animal life of today.

Late Jurassic 157–146 mya
Supercontinent beginning to break up, dry inland, moist climates by coasts.

Early Cretaceous 146–97 mya
Continents drifting into separate landmasses, plant life as in Triassic and Jurassic periods.

Late Cretaceous 97–65 mya
Separate continents, each with its own animal life, and plants like modern types.

COELOPHYSIS—hunting in packs

Like a wolf pack, the small group of agile creatures patters along the dry stream bed. Each one carries its big head low, its keen eyes looking ahead for food. The animals' slim bodies are each balanced on long birdlike hind legs by a stiff tail. They hold their strong-clawed hands folded close to the chest.

Coelophysis was one of the earliest hunting dinosaurs. Somewhere along this stream course lies their prey—one of the big hippopotamus-like plant-eating reptiles that died out in the Late Triassic Period as the dinosaurs took over.

We know that *Coelophysis* moved about in packs because a mass of their skeletons was found in a quarry in New Mexico. A whole pack must have died together. Maybe they were all washed away in a flash flood, or else they gathered round a water hole in a desert oasis until it dried up completely and they died of thirst. The second possibility seems likely, since some of the skeletons had the remains of baby *Coelophysis* in the stomach area. So harsh were the conditions that the adult dinosaurs were forced to eat the young of their own kind in order to survive.

In Connecticut, sandstone rocks from the Early Jurassic Period are full of the three-toed footprints of *Coelophysis,* or of some animal very similar. Before people knew anything about dinosaurs, these footprints were thought to have been made by birds of some kind.

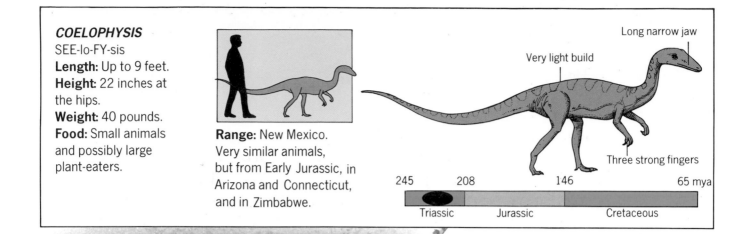

COELOPHYSIS
SEE-lo-FY-sis
Length: Up to 9 feet.
Height: 22 inches at the hips.
Weight: 40 pounds.
Food: Small animals and possibly large plant-eaters.

Range: New Mexico. Very similar animals, but from Early Jurassic, in Arizona and Connecticut, and in Zimbabwe.

Long narrow jaw

Very light build

Three strong fingers

245	208	146	65 mya
Triassic	Jurassic	Cretaceous	

◁ The *Coelophysis* pack slinks along the dry stream bed as the startled flying reptile *Icarosaurus* glides away. *Coelophysis* had teeth like carving knives. Its narrow flexible snout allowed it to grab small active prey.

△ Modern wolves hunt their prey in packs, probably as *Coelophysis* did. A large pack can bring down prey bigger than any single wolf. Working alone, each wolf has to be content with catching small animals to eat.

HETERODONTOSAURUS—varied teeth

Most modern reptiles, such as lizards and crocodiles, have teeth that are all the same size. It is really only the mammals, such as cats, dogs, rodents, and monkeys, that have teeth organized into killing teeth, biting teeth, grinding teeth, and so on. Some of the dinosaurs, however, had different-sized teeth, each with special functions.

Heterodontosaurus (the name means "reptile with different-sized teeth") was one of the first of these. It had sharp teeth at the front for cutting off the leaves that it ate, long fangs at each side probably for breaking stems, and broad teeth at the back for grinding food. This is the same kind of tooth arrangement that people have! Some specimens seem to lack the fangs. Maybe only the males had them and they used them for fighting.

Apart from the teeth, *Heterodontosaurus* looked very much like any other primitive two-footed plant-eating dinosaur. It would have spent most of its time on its hind legs balanced by its long tail, like the meat-eaters of the time. If you had been around, you would easily have been able to tell a two-footed plant-eater from a meat-eater. The plant-eater would have had a much heavier body, as it needed a bigger intestine to digest its tough food. Also, nearly all the two-footed plant-eaters had cheek-pouches, to hold the food while chewing it. The meat-eaters would have had crocodile-like jaws. Like all the later two-footed plant-eaters, *Heterodontosaurus* had a horny beak at the front of its mouth. Its five-fingered hands had a big-clawed thumb that could grasp the plants on which it fed.

▷ With its teeth of different sizes, a *Heterodontosaurus* scavenges for food around a dead tree at the edge of the Early Jurassic desert.

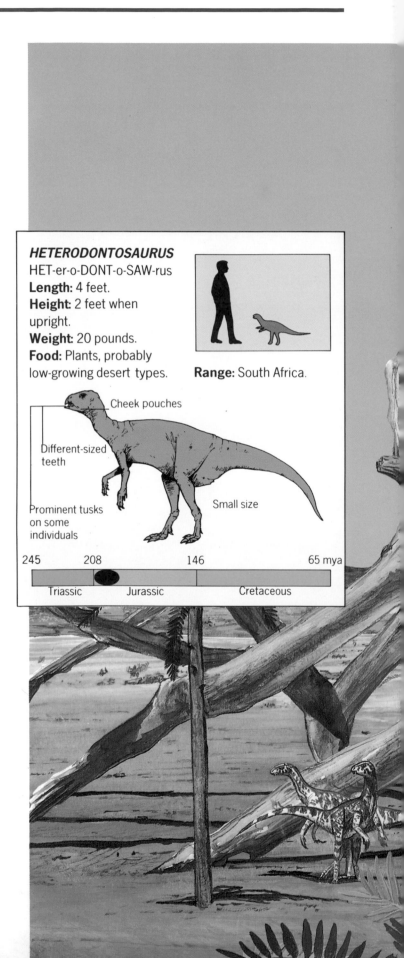

HETERODONTOSAURUS
HET-er-o-DONT-o-SAW-rus
Length: 4 feet.
Height: 2 feet when upright.
Weight: 20 pounds.
Food: Plants, probably low-growing desert types.

Range: South Africa.

Cheek pouches

Different-sized teeth

Prominent tusks on some individuals

Small size

245	208	146	65 mya
Triassic	Jurassic	Cretaceous	

▷ *Heterodontosaurus* skeletons have been found curled up together. Perhaps they slept through the drier seasons of the year in burrows, as do some modern desert animals like these Cape ground squirrels.

SCUTELLOSAURUS—an armor coat

As the Age of Dinosaurs progressed, the plant-eating dinosaurs developed all kinds of techniques for escaping from the meat-eaters. Some became fast runners. Others became armored. *Scutellosaurus,* found in Early Jurassic rocks in North America, appears to be one of the first species that was both fast and armored.

It was lightly built, and although its hind legs were not as long as those of some other plant-eaters of the time, it was well balanced at the hips. Its tail was thin and very long—one and a half times the length of the rest of the body. *Scutellosaurus* could easily scamper away from danger. By comparison to the hind legs, the animal's forelimbs were quite long, so it looks as if *Scutellosaurus* spent most of its time down on all fours. It had tiny five-fingered clawed hands.

The most remarkable feature of this dinosaur was its armor. Parallel rows of bony studs covered its back and formed a spiky ridge from its skull to the tip of its tail. When attacked, *Scutellosaurus* may have crouched down in the soil presenting the armor to its attacker. Any large meat-eater that picked up the animal would get an extremely unpleasant bony mouthful.

Apart from these features, *Scutellosaurus* seems to have been very lizardlike. It was no bigger than some of the larger lizards that are alive today, and its head was quite unlike that of the other two-footed plant-eaters. It lacked the cheek pouches that most of the others had. Instead, it had widely spaced leaf-shaped teeth that it used to shred its plant food. Modern iguana lizards have similar teeth for exactly the same job.

▷ The long-tailed knobby *Scutellosaurus* surveys the landscape, keeping an eye open for enemies. If you saw it scuttling across dry rocks or disappearing into undergrowth, you would probably think that you were looking at some kind of lizard. *Scutellosaurus* means "reptile with little shields."

◁ In the modern world the armor of the pangolin probably comes closest to that of *Scutellosaurus.* Like the little dinosaur, the pangolin can run quite quickly when it is chased by a meat-eating animal. But if it is caught, its armor plates give it a great deal of protection.

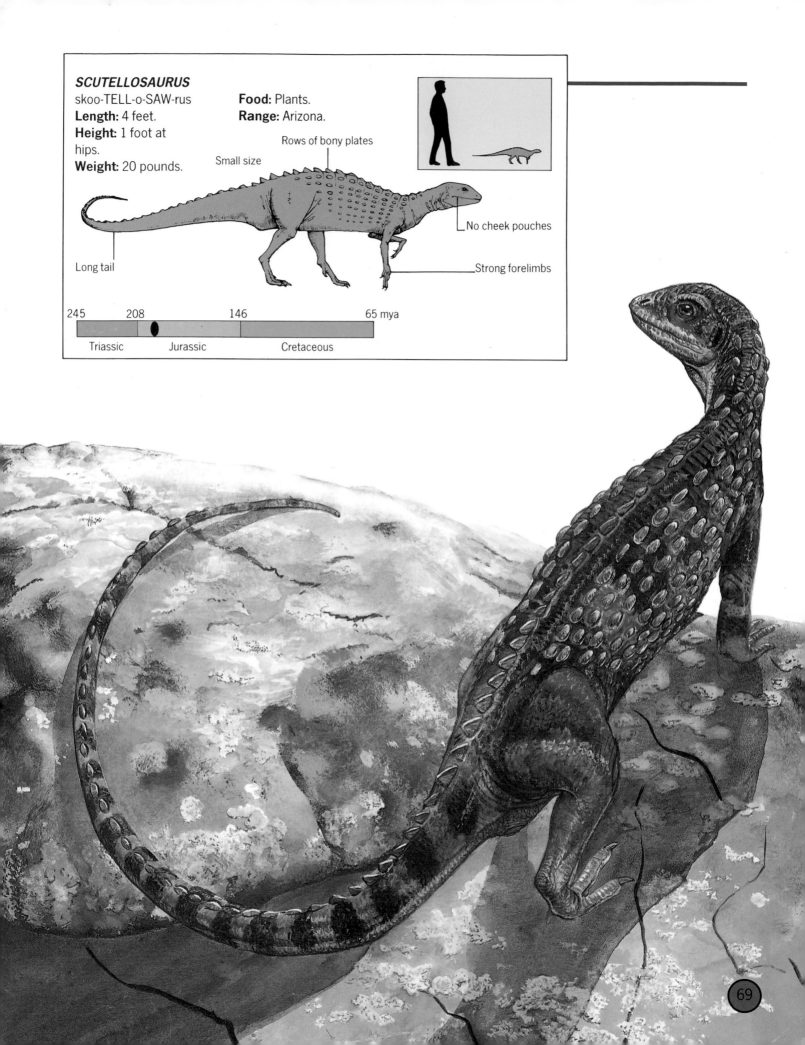

SCUTELLOSAURUS
skoo-TELL-o-SAW-rus
Length: 4 feet.
Height: 1 foot at hips.
Weight: 20 pounds.

Food: Plants.
Range: Arizona.

Small size

Rows of bony plates

No cheek pouches

Long tail

Strong forelimbs

245	208	146	65 mya
Triassic	Jurassic	Cretaceous	

SCELIDOSAURUS—heavy and spiky

It is the Early Jurassic Period. A low upland ridge stretches across the area that now lies between Wales and Belgium. The vegetation that grows on the hills is the same green all over—the green of conifers and tree ferns. There are no flowers anywhere. At times big-headed *Dimorphodon* pterosaurs fly in the clear sky. In a valley, the ferns are pushed aside by a smallish knobbly-looking dinosaur, *Scelidosaurus,* as it lumbers down to the stream to drink.

Big meat-eating dinosaurs were around in Early Jurassic times. The plant-eaters had to beware and keep out of their way. At about this time the big plant-eaters began to develop armor. *Scelidosaurus* was one of the first of the species of armored dinosaurs.

At about the size of a sheep or small cow, *Scelidosaurus* was not really a big animal. However, it was obviously one that was too heavy to run away from its enemies. It used its armor to defend itself. The armor consisted of rows of bony knobs set into the skin of the back, running from the back of the skull down to the tip of the tail. In life, these knobs would have been sheathed in horn and were probably rather spiky. *Scelidosaurus* had legs that were fairly stout. It went around on all fours.

The main groups of armored dinosaurs did not evolve until the Late Jurassic and Early

SCELIDOSAURUS
skel-IDE-o-SAW-rus
Length: 13 feet.
Height: 3-4 feet at hips.
Weight: 500 pounds.

Food: Plants.
Range: Southern England, with closely related animals in Portugal and Germany.

Rows of conical plates on back

Beak

Cheek pouches

Four-footed stance

245   208   146   65 mya

Triassic   Jurassic   Cretaceous

◁ The armored dinosaur *Scelidosaurus* approaches the Early Jurassic seashore. It would have carried its head close to the ground to feed on low-growing plants such as ferns, horsetails, and cycads.

Cretaceous periods. Scientists have always thought that *Scelidosaurus* must have been the ancestor of the later types. The two great armored groups were the stegosaurs, with upright plates and spines on the back, and the ankylosaurs, with horizontal shields and spikes pointing out sideways. It seems most likely that *Scelidosaurus* belonged to a group that evolved into the ankylosaurs. One reason for this thinking is that *Scelidosaurus* had its skull encased in bony plates, as had the later ankylosaurs but not the stegosaurs. But we have found no fossils of armored dinosaurs from the 40 million years between *Scelidosaurus* and the later armored types.

▽ The Indian rhinoceros is a large, armored, stoutly built plant-eater. Its armor consists of thick folds of lumpy skin. It relies on its armor in battles with other rhinoceroses for territory or for mates.

ORNITHOLESTES—a small, swift hunter

On the Late Jurassic plains of western North America, herds of huge plant-eaters like *Apatosaurus* and *Brachiosaurus,* and the armored giants like *Stegosaurus,* were stalked and killed by mighty meat-eaters, among them *Allosaurus*. However, not all the dinosaurs there at that time were large monsters. There were also lightweight, nimble little meat-eaters like *Ornitholestes*.

The small mammals of the time, along with the lizards and lizardlike animals, and even hatchling dinosaurs, would have been fair game for any small jackal-sized hunter. *Ornitholestes* was just such a creature, and its light build would also have given it the speed to chase down startled lizards or to escape from enraged adult dinosaurs who found their nests raided.

Ornitholestes had a body shape like that of the big meat-eaters but on a small scale. In fact, it was probably closely related to the local giant, *Allosaurus*. It could use its hands well. Each hand had two very long fingers and one quite short. *Ornitholestes* could probably have used the short finger like a thumb for grasping. All three fingers had strong claws.

The skull of *Ornitholestes* was very short, which is unusual for the smaller meat-eating dinosaurs, and its lower jaw was deep and strong. This may mean that the animal killed its prey by a strong bite, as do cats, rather than by pulling it to bits with its claws.

Ornitholestes means "bird-robber," but there is no evidence to show that it really did catch and eat birds.

△ The modern secretary bird of Africa is like *Ornitholestes*. It is a swift long-legged ground hunter that chases small mammals and reptiles through the undergrowth in the same way that we believe *Ornitholestes* did in Jurassic times.

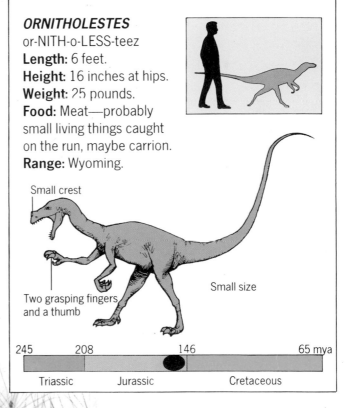

ORNITHOLESTES
or-NITH-o-LESS-teez
Length: 6 feet.
Height: 16 inches at hips.
Weight: 25 pounds.
Food: Meat—probably small living things caught on the run, maybe carrion.
Range: Wyoming.

Small crest

Two grasping fingers and a thumb

Small size

245	208	146	65 mya
Triassic	Jurassic	Cretaceous	

◁ *Ornitholestes* snatches a young crocodile from its nest to eat. Having killed its prey, *Ornitholestes* probably swallowed it whole. *Ornitholestes*'s small size meant that it could hunt small fast-moving prey that was not available to the larger dinosaurs of the region.

ELAPHROSAURUS—a birdlike meat-eater

This dinosaur was like a cheetah—long and lean, built for speed—but it ran on its hind legs. It lived on the wooded coastal plain of Tanzania in East Africa in the Late Jurassic Period. Its neighbors were the huge long-necked plant-eater *Brachiosaurus* and the stegosaur *Kentrosaurus*. These it left well alone. Instead, it hunted the small or medium-sized plant-eaters such as *Dryosaurus*, a close relative of *Hypsilophodon*.

The lightness of *Elaphrosaurus*'s build and parts of its skeleton, particularly the front limbs, make us think that it was related to the small meat-eating dinosaurs of Triassic and Early Jurassic times, such as *Coelophysis*.

However, its size and its leg bones seem to show that it was an early member of the birdlike dinosaurs, such as *Avimimus*, which became common later.

An incomplete skeleton was discovered in Tanzania in the 1920s. Since then, odd bones possibly from *Elaphrosaurus* have been found all over northern Africa. In the 1980s, an arm bone that seems to have belonged to a front limb of this beast was found in Late Jurassic rocks of Wyoming in the United States. This suggests that *Elaphrosaurus*, as well as *Brachiosaurus* and the stegosaurs, spread all over the world before the continents broke up in the middle of the Age of Dinosaurs.

▽ Long-bodied, swift-moving *Elaphrosaurus* must have pursued the agile plant-eater *Dryosaurus* through the woods and thickets of Late Jurassic Tanzania, dodging to keep its prey in sight as it ran it down.

△ On the modern plains of Tanzania the cheetah runs down the gazelle on which it preys. Both animals are built for speed. Sometimes the cheetah wins the chase, and sometimes the gazelle. Dinosaur chases would have had similar endings.

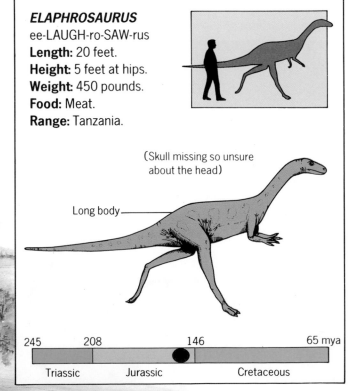

ELAPHROSAURUS
ee-LAUGH-ro-SAW-rus
Length: 20 feet.
Height: 5 feet at hips.
Weight: 450 pounds.
Food: Meat.
Range: Tanzania.

(Skull missing so unsure about the head)

Long body

245	208	146	65 mya
Triassic	Jurassic		Cretaceous

KENTROSAURUS—with unusual features

When we think of stegosaurs, we usually picture the massive *Stegosaurus* itself. However, the stegosaurs were a group of dinosaurs of various shapes and sizes. Some of them were quite small. *Kentrosaurus* was only about the size of a large cow. But it was not only its size that was special. The arrangement of plates on its back was totally different from that of *Stegosaurus*. Instead of a double row of broad slabs, *Kentrosaurus* had plates that were so narrow they could be considered spines. Its name means "pointy reptile." Small and leaflike over the neck, the spines grew tall and narrow over the hips and tail. There was also a pair of sideways-pointing spines in the region of the hips or shoulders.

Scientists disagree over the exact purpose of the stegosaurs' plates or spines. Many think that the big broad plates of *Stegosaurus* were used for controlling the heat of the animal. The plates and spines of *Kentrosaurus* would seem to be far too narrow for this job. Maybe *Kentrosaurus*'s smaller size meant that it did not need such a complicated temperature control system. Its plates and spines were probably used only as armor. Only when the big stegosaurs, like *Stegosaurus*, evolved, did these armor spines develop into heat exchangers.

A second brain or a powerpack?

Another dinosaur feature that experts disagree about is a cavity, or hollow space, that lies between the hip bones of the stegosaurs. It was once thought that this housed a second brain that could control movement of the hind legs and the tail. It is more likely to have held a gland or organ—a mass of body tissue—that supplied energy to the hindparts of the animal in an emergency.

▷ *Kentrosaurus* browses in the thicket, protected from the fierce meat-eaters of the time by its bladelike plates and sharp spines. Scientists at first thought the sideways-pointing spines were over the hip, but discoveries in China have shown that they were over the shoulder as shown here. *Kentrosaurus* lived in the wooded riversides of Tanzania in Late Jurassic times.

KENTROSAURUS
KENT-ro-SAW-rus
Length: up to 15 feet.
Height: 3-6 feet.
Weight: 1,000 pounds.
Food: Plants.
Range: Tanzania.

Narrow plates on neck and back

Small head

Beak

Cheek pouches

Long spines on tail

245	208	146	65 mya
Triassic	Jurassic	Cretaceous	

COMPSOGNATHUS—lizard-chaser

A little chicken-sized creature, scampering along a shoreline, disturbing clouds of sandflies from the mounds of seaweed.

Not the image we usually have of a dinosaur, is it? Yet this is *Compsognathus*, the smallest and lightest dinosaur that we know. It must have looked very much like a naked chicken. In build and structure it was very much like the first bird, *Archaeopteryx*, which lived at the same time and in the same place. This was the Late Jurassic, and the place was the island group that lay scattered across the shallow sea that covered much of northern Europe at that time.

The skeletons of *Compsognathus* discovered so far exist as fossils in well-formed limestone rock that developed in shallow waters long ago. The limestone was formed so perfectly that it has preserved details of the dinosaur's way of life. The most famous skeleton, found in Germany, is possibly that of a female. It still had the bones of the animal's last meal in its stomach cavity. It was a fast-moving long-tailed lizard like a modern iguana. *Compsognathus* probably ate other small animals, too, such as insects and early mammals.

Now we can picture its last activities. While searching for somewhere to lay her eggs, the *Compsognathus* sees the lizard run out into the sunlight of the beach. This is too good a chance of a meal to miss. On her long hind legs she scampers after it and, after a short chase, she seizes it in her little teeth, kills it, and swallows it whole. Maybe the chase took her so far down the beach that a wave caught her and she drowned. Eventually she sank to the bottom of the sea and was fossilized.

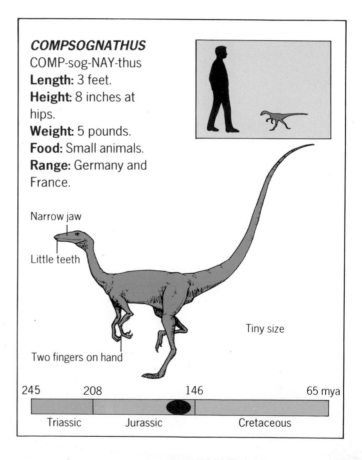

COMPSOGNATHUS
COMP-sog-NAY-thus
Length: 3 feet.
Height: 8 inches at hips.
Weight: 5 pounds.
Food: Small animals.
Range: Germany and France.

Narrow jaw

Little teeth

Two fingers on hand

Tiny size

245	208	146	65 mya
Triassic	Jurassic	Cretaceous	

▽ Imagine a chicken
without any feathers. Then
give it a long tail and a
toothy mouth. This is what
Compsognathus looked
like. One skeleton of the
first bird, *Archaeopteryx*,
was thought to have been
that of *Compsognathus*
until someone noticed
there were impressions of
feathers around it.

HYPSILOPHODON—small but speedy

A small plant-eating dinosaur, built for speed so that it could escape the big meat-eaters by running away across open ground. That describes *Hypsilophodon*. For a plant-eater it was very lightly built and well-balanced at the hips. The legs were long and graceful, with short thighs and particularly long shin bones and toes. Most of the leg muscles worked on the short thigh bone. This meant that all the weight was concentrated at the thigh and the hip, and the rest of the leg was lightweight. An arrangement like this meant that the legs could be moved quickly, showing that *Hypsilophodon* was a running animal.

Apart from that, *Hypsilophodon* must have looked like a little *Iguanodon,* the classic big plant-eating dinosaur of Early Cretaceous southern England. A sharp narrow beak would have allowed *Hypsilophodon* to select and nip out the tastiest pieces from the shoots and leaves on which it fed. It would have used its chisel-like cheek teeth to chop up the food while holding it in its cheek pouches.

The arms of *Hypsilophodon* were quite long, although shorter than the legs, with hands each having five stubby fingers. These would have been ideal for grabbing and pulling food toward the mouth. Like most two-footed dinosaurs, *Hypsilophodon* had a long tail that was stiffened by bony tendons and held straight out behind. It was used as a balancing pole while running.

On the Isle of Wight, off southern England, is a layer of rock packed with *Hypsilophodon* skeletons. Evidently a disaster overcame a herd of them. Probably they were crossing coastal mudflats and were cut off by the tide, or they were trapped in quicksand. Whatever killed them was something they could not run away from fast enough.

Suited for a new food source

The earliest of the horned dinosaurs lived in Late Cretaceous Mongolia, just where *Psittacosaurus* lived. Later, they would have migrated across to North America, the home of the great horn-bearers of the end of the Cretaceous Period.

At about this time, all over the world the vegetation was changing. The cycads and fernlike plants were dying out and being replaced by the flowering plants that we know today. The big beak of *Psittacosaurus* may have evolved to cope with the tough woody stems and to crack the hard seeds and nuts of these new plants.

STYGIMOLOCH—herd-living bonehead

Imagine this dinosaur popping its head up through the undergrowth to look at you! A head as big as a soccer ball, with a dome on top and surrounded by spikes and horns. Yet, like most other alarming-looking animals, *Stygimoloch* was a harmless plant-eater.

It was a member of a group of dinosaurs that we call the boneheads. These were mostly sheep-sized animals, although the biggest species grew to about 25 feet long. In bodily build they were much like the usual two-footed plant-eaters. But in the structure of the head, they were quite different. The top of the skull was very thick. In some species, including *Stygimoloch,* this thickening was enlarged into a distinct dome. It must have seemed as if each animal's skull contained a large brain. However, it was nearly all bone, and bone that was thickened in such a way as to make it extemely strong.

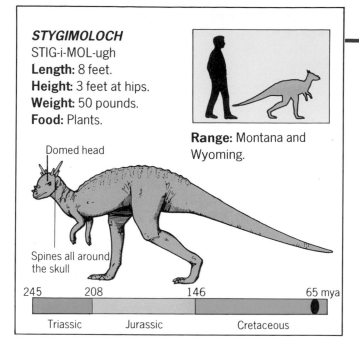

STYGIMOLOCH
STIG-i-MOL-ugh
Length: 8 feet.
Height: 3 feet at hips.
Weight: 50 pounds.
Food: Plants.

Range: Montana and Wyoming.

Domed head

Spines all around the skull

245   208   146   65 mya

Triassic   Jurassic   Cretaceous

◁ A male *Stygimoloch* rests in the shade after a head-butting contest with another male. Dome-headed dinosaurs probably had such fights to decide who would lead the herd, just as male mountain goats do today. The boneheads may also have been mountain dwellers. Most of their remains that we know consist of skulls that had been washed down from the mountains and badly worn by water before being fossilized.

▽ The modern horned lizard, the so-called horned toad, has spines around its head as did *Stygimoloch*. Like the lizard's, the spines of *Stygimoloch* may have kept off meat-eaters.

Little brains, lots of brawn

What would a dome on the head have been used for? It seems likely that the boneheads lived in herds, and that the big males fought for leadership of the herds by head-butting one another, just as male sheep and goats do today. The bones of the neck and back were arranged to withstand the shock when the head was used as a battering ram. In *Stygimoloch,* the domed head was surrounded by spines, no doubt to make the head look bigger and more frightening. (To us it may have looked like some sort of monster.) Perhaps *Stygimoloch* rivals did not charge and crash with one another but instead locked horns and pushed.

The hips of the boneheads were very wide, and it is possible that this means these species of dinosaurs gave birth to live young rather than laying eggs.

OVIRAPTOR—fierce and fast egg-robber

Do you eat eggs for breakfast? There is plenty of protein in an egg—good nourishing food. Most of the dinosaurs laid eggs, and so during dinosaur times there must have been a great number of good meals lying around in the form of eggs. One feature of evolution is that wherever there is a new food supply, something will evolve to feed on it. We think that *Oviraptor* was a dinosaur that evolved to eat the eggs of others.

The first skeleton of an *Oviraptor* to be found was lying near a nest full of eggs of *Protoceratops,* one of the first horned dinosaurs. The animal must have been buried in a sandstorm while it was robbing the nest.

The head of *Oviraptor* was very odd. The skull was extremely short with a deep beak.

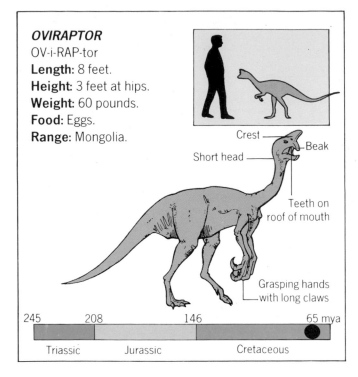

OVIRAPTOR
OV-i-RAP-tor
Length: 8 feet.
Height: 3 feet at hips.
Weight: 60 pounds.
Food: Eggs.
Range: Mongolia.

Crest — Beak
Short head
Teeth on roof of mouth
Grasping hands with long claws

245	208	146	65 mya
Triassic	Jurassic	Cretaceous	

△ There are birds around today that eat the eggs of others, like this crow about to eat a goose's egg. We know this because we see it happen. When it comes to dinosaurs, though, we can get an idea of what they ate by the shapes of the mouth and teeth.

The only teeth were a pair high up on the roof of the mouth. A mouth of this shape would have been perfect for cracking open eggs. *Oviraptor* had a tall crest just like that of a cassowary, a bird that lives today in Australia and New Guinea. The eyes were at each side of the head, to allow it to keep a lookout all round for danger while it fed. The hands were short, with three strong-clawed fingers shaped so that they could hold big eggs.

The body of *Oviraptor* was built like that of the small meat-eating dinosaurs, so that it would have looked a lot like a large bird. The long legs would have allowed it to run off when danger threatened, but the big claws and the strong beak would have been formidable weapons if it came to a fight.

▷ Crouched over a dinosaur nest by moonlight, *Oviraptor* watches for the owner. *Oviraptor* evolved as an egg-eater. With its flexible hands it could hold an egg while using its deep beak and special teeth to break through the shell. It then gobbled up the contents.

AVIMIMUS— built like a bird

Avimimus, or "bird-mimic," was the most birdlike of all dinosaurs. The eyes were big, like an owl's. The skull was deep and narrow, like a pheasant's. The legs were long, resembling those of a roadrunner; the toes were short like an ostrich's. The arms could be tucked back against the body, just as wings can. In fact, the whole beast was so birdlike that some paleontologists think that it evolved from the first types of birds, or at least some earlier flying creature. They show the dinosaur covered with feathers. It was no bird, though.

The hips of *Avimimus* were typical dinosaur hips and its arms were too small to have been wings. The tail is missing from the only known skeleton of *Avimimus,* and some scientists think that it did not have a proper tail at all, just a bunch of long feathers as birds do. But most others do not believe this since the hips are very broad and show where strong tail muscles were attached.

Although *Avimimus* was related to the small meat-eating dinosaurs, it seems more likely that it ate plants. This is similar to the way that bears and pandas are related to the

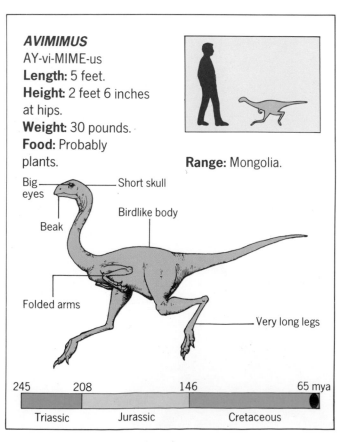

◁ The modern roadrunner has a pair of legs similar in structure and shape to those of *Avimimus.* It can fly, but prefers to run, just as the smaller dinosaurs did.

AVIMIMUS
AY-vi-MIME-us
Length: 5 feet.
Height: 2 feet 6 inches at hips.
Weight: 30 pounds.
Food: Probably plants.

Range: Mongolia.

Big eyes — — Short skull

Beak

Birdlike body

Folded arms

Very long legs

245	208	146	65 mya
Triassic	Jurassic	Cretaceous	

meat-eating dogs and cats, but they eat mostly plants. *Avimimus* had a completely different diet from its cousins. Its broad beak, like that of an ostrich, seems to have been adapted for eating low-growing vegetable matter. The long ostrichlike neck would have allowed it to reach down to the ground. A saw edge on the beak enabled it to remove plants easily from the soil.

It was clearly a running animal with legs as long as its body and neck. It must have grazed on open plains and taken to its heels as soon as one of its meat-eating relatives appeared.

Avimimus lived on the open plains of Late Cretaceous Mongolia. There, at the same time, lived the egg-stealer *Oviraptor*. There were also small meat-eaters that were fast on their feet and armed with killing claws. Such animals as *Troodon* and *Velociraptor* would have given chase, but *Avimimus* would have given them a good run.

▽ *Avimimus* sprints across the Late Cretaceous plains of central Asia, its head bobbing and its arms tucked into its body. Built for speed, it would have outrun most of the meat-eating hunting dinosaurs of the time.

The Age of Dinosaurs

The first dinosaurs appeared about 225 million years ago (mya for short) in what scientists call the Late Triassic Period. They thrived through the following Jurassic Period and died out at the end of the Cretaceous Period 65 million years ago. During this time, geography, climate, and vegetation, or plant life, were constantly changing—as shown in these dinosaur scenes.

Triassic 245–208 mya
A single giant landmass or supercontinent, mostly desert conditions, tree ferns, and conifers.

Early and Middle Jurassic 208–157 mya Supercontinent, shallow seas, moist climate, tree ferns, conifers, and cycads.

FOUR

A Closer Look

They have been dead for 65 million years. All that is left of them are a few bones, and those have been turned to stone, or fossils, by the natural workings of the Earth. How, then, do we know about the dinosaurs, these former inhabitants of our world? How do we know about what their bodies were like, about how they lived, and about what kind of family life they had?

We can use our imaginations. But our best understanding will be based on scientific evidence. There are all kinds of clues that can give us a good picture of ancient life. Over the past 150 years, since dinosaurs were first recognized as an animal group, the dinosaur hunters and the scientists who study the fossils have been putting these clues together. They find information in the rocks that contain the dinosaur fossils, in the markings or scars on the bones themselves, and from comparisons that can be made between creatures of the past and living animals.

Slowly, bit by bit, they have been building up a realistic picture of these great creatures of our early world. They have reconstructed the intestines, or guts, inside the rib cages, put flesh on the bones, covered the bodies with skin, and placed the animals in the landscapes they inhabited. The scientists have almost made the dinosaurs live again for us.

Late Jurassic 157–146 mya
Supercontinent beginning to break up, dry inland, moist climates by coasts.

Early Cretaceous 146–97 mya
Continents drifting into separate landmasses, plant life as in Triassic and Jurassic periods.

Late Cretaceous 97–65 mya
Separate continents, each with its own animal life, and plants like modern types.

DINOSAURS WERE REAL

The Sun beats down on the dusty plain in the middle of the continent that we now call Asia. Through the scattering of conifer trees wanders a herd of the long-necked plant-eating dinosaur *Shunosaurus*. It is the end of the wet season, and the animals are migrating to find new feeding grounds. A big male steps out in front, leading the way. The youngest of the herd stay with the main group, protected by the presence of their elders. Overhead, a small flock of the toothy-jawed pterosaur *Angustinaripterus* flies towards rivers and lakes that are well stocked with fish.

▷ Using bits of evidence, we can create a picture of a herd of dinosaurs migrating through its landscape. As scientists discover new clues of life in the past, our picture comes into sharper focus.

∇ In size and feeding habits, the elephants are the nearest creatures that we have to the big plant-eating dinosaurs. The way that elephants behave, such as migrating in herds, gives us an idea of how the ancient dinosaurs may have lived.

How do we know these events occurred? All that we are likely to see of *Shunosaurus* is a collection of fossilized bones in a museum. Did this dinosaur really behave in this way? Was the landscape truly as is shown here? Did these pterosaurs, flying reptiles, actually live at the same time and in the same place?

Paleontology—the study of ancient life— is full of such questions. Our knowledge of the world of the past is something like the result of a detective story. Everything that we know about it has to be pieced together until the full picture emerges. Just as important as the fossilized bones themselves are the rocks in which they are found. The type of rock can reveal what the environment was like—for instance, whether the climate was hot or cold, wet or dry.

The fossils contained in the rocks can tell us what other animals and what plants lived at the time. By comparing these with similar present-day living things that we know behave in certain ways or only live in certain places, the paleontologist may help us to understand how dinosaurs lived and behaved, and died, in ancient times.

DINOSAUR ANATOMY

A dinosaur, when it was alive, consisted of more than just the bones that we see in the museum. As in any other vertebrate, an animal with a backbone, the bony skeleton was just the support—the scaffolding that held the creature up. The rest consisted of soft squishy parts. First, there were the muscles that worked on the bones, pulling them like levers and allowing the animal to move.

Cutaway view of the anatomy of *Chasmosaurus*, a plant-eater

Dinosaur skin

When a dinosaur was buried quickly in mud, the mud sometimes took the impression of the skin. When the mud turned to rock, the impression was preserved, so we can see what the skin was like.

The intestines processed the food the animal ate to produce the raw material for building its muscles. The lungs took in oxygen from the air to provide the fuel to keep the muscles and the body working. The brain controlled the actions of the whole body. Next there was the nervous system, a communications network that sent messages from the brain to the body's different parts. The eyes, the ears, and the nose allowed the dinosaur to sense what was going on around it and send the information to the brain. Finally, there was the skin that provided the outer covering for the whole animal.

Dinosaur droppings

Droppings are undigested food material released from the body. Those of an ancient animal are sometimes preserved as fossils. If we know which animal produced them, we can tell something about the food it ate and what its digestive system was like. To date, though, dinosaur droppings have not been studied in much detail.

Dinosaur muscles

If we look at a fossil dinosaur bone, we can see the scars and knobs to which the muscles were attached. From this we can work out how big the muscles were, how they were arranged on the skeleton, and thus how the skeletal joints worked and how the animal used them to move, stand, or reach for food.

Dinosaur skull
About half of all dinosaurs are known from complete fossil skulls. But often the skulls were crushed or lost completely.

Dinosaur teeth
Grinding teeth show a vegetable diet. Stabbing and flesh-tearing teeth are the mark of a meat-eater.

Dinosaur bones
A full set of bones, joined together as a skeleton allowing body movement, is the best guide to the look of an ancient animal.

Dinosaur guts
We can get an idea of how much food the digestive system of a dinosaur held from the volume inside its rib cage and the space in front of and below its hips. Plant-eaters like the *Chasmosaurus* illustrated here have bigger stomachs and intestines than those of meat-eaters, to digest lots of tough vegetable material.

Dinosaur feet
The best evidence for the shape and structure of a dinosaur's feet are its footprints. A set of footprints tells us how the animal walked and perhaps the speed at which it ran, and whether it went around alone or in herds. But it is often difficult to tell exactly which type of dinosaur made the prints.

Built like other beasts
All this soft matter decayed away soon after the animal's death. Often it was eaten by other animals, perhaps even other dinosaurs. Usually it was only the bones that were left behind and could become fossils.

We know that all dinosaurs had a full set of these soft parts since, as living creatures, they would not have been able to survive without them. There are no whole dinosaurs whose anatomy, or body structure, we can examine, but if we look closely enough at dinosaur remains, there are often plenty of clues that tell us what they were like.

MEAT OR PLANT?

Some animals eat plants, others eat meat—usually the flesh of the plant-eaters! In the vast range of dinosaurs there were both meat-eaters and plant-eaters. The meat-eating dinosaurs probably evolved first, preying on other types of reptiles. The plant-eaters developed from them.

As a rule, the meat-eaters were two-footed animals, standing and moving around on their hind limbs. This allowed them to run quickly and catch their prey. They had big slashing teeth and grasping hands that were held forward, and were balanced at the hips by a heavy tail. All the meat-eaters, from chicken-sized *Compsognathus* to 40-foot-long *Tyrannosaurus,* followed this design.

▷ The largest modern lizard, the Komodo dragon, reaches lengths of 10 feet. This is smaller than most of the meat-eating dinosaurs but its jagged-edged teeth, long claws, and jaws give us a good idea of how they ate.

Plant-eater

If you had seen a two-footed plant-eating dinosaur, you would not have mistaken it for a meat-eater. Its big stomach and intestines would have given it a rather pot-bellied appearance. The head would have cheek pouches to hold the vegetable matter while chewing. It would have had a beak at the front of its mouth for nipping off twigs and leaves, and its teeth would have been broad and flat-topped for grinding.

Two-footed plant-eater

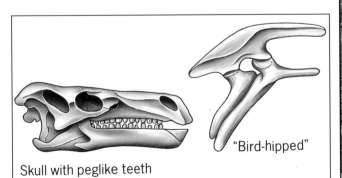

Skull with peglike teeth

"Bird-hipped"

Plant-eating dinosaurs needed much bigger intestines than meat-eating ones in order to process more food. When the first plant-eaters evolved, their heavy guts unbalanced them. The later types evolved to move around on all fours. They developed long necks that enabled them to reach around for food, and the basic shape of the long-necked plant-eating dinosaur, such as *Apatosaurus,* evolved.

Meanwhile another group of plant-eaters was developing with the big guts now slung between the hind legs. These dinosaurs could still balance and walk around on two feet. *Iguanodon* and *Parasaurolophus* were two-footed plant-eating dinosaurs. Some of these two-footed species developed armor. Again this increased their weight and they took up a four-footed way of life. Plant-eaters of this type included *Stegosaurus, Triceratops,* and *Euoplocephalus.*

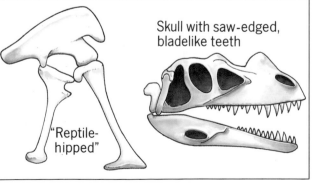

Two-footed meat-eater

Skull with saw-edged, bladelike teeth

"Reptile-hipped"

Meat-eater

A two-footed, lizard-hipped, meat-eating dinosaur of the same size as the two-footed plant-eater opposite would have been much slimmer and more lightly built. Its head would have been much larger, and the long gash of its mouth would have shown off its series of bladelike killing teeth. Most meat-eaters had fewer than five fingers on the hand, whereas the plant-eaters had either four or five fingers.

WARM- OR COLD-BLOODED?

Modern reptiles are cold-blooded. This does not mean that their blood is cold all the time but that it stays at the same temperature as their surroundings. If the weather is hot, they become hot, and if the weather is cold, they become cold. By moving between sunny and shady places, reptiles can control their body temperature.

Mammals and birds, on the other hand, are warm-blooded. This means that they can regulate the temperature of their bodies and keep themselves at the same temperature in all conditions. Hot weather does not upset them much, and they can stay active in cool weather. This lifestyle uses up lots of energy, and a warm-blooded animal needs about ten times as much food as a cold-blooded type.

Dinosaurs were reptiles, and so it was always thought that they were cold-blooded. But in the 1970s some scientists began to think that they may have actually been warm-blooded. Evidence came from several points: the way the dinosaurs stood—straight-legged like mammals; from their big rib cages that could have held mammal-like hearts and lungs; and from their bones that contained channels for fast blood circulation as in warm-blooded animals' bones.

▷ If a small meat-eating dinosaur such as *Velociraptor* had been cold-blooded, it would have had a skin similar to a lizard's.

▽ If *Velociraptor* had been warm-blooded, it may have been covered with fur or feathers as part of its temperature-regulation system.

If a small fast-running dinosaur such as *Velociraptor* or *Dromiceiomimus*, above, had been warm-blooded, it would have been able to run about for a long time without tiring. If it had been cold-blooded, after any burst of activity it would have had to spend some time cooling off and resting before it was able to exert itself again. *Dromiceiomimus* ran after its prey at 40 mph.

Other scientists still regarded dinosaurs as being cold-blooded. They could not believe that a big, long-necked, plant-eating dinosaur could possibly have eaten enough food to fuel a warm-blooded lifestyle. And their bodies were so massive that they would have been able to keep in their heat in cool weather.

More recent studies of dinosaur bones suggest that these animals were neither warm-blooded like mammals nor cold-blooded like reptiles, but something in between. Meat-eaters may have been able to regulate their temperatures, but not to such an extent as modern mammals and birds. Big plant-eaters did not seem to have had much control over their temperatures, but they were not as cold-blooded as modern reptiles.

Heating and cooling
A big, long-necked plant-eating dinosaur like *Apatosaurus* would have had such a massive body that it could have kept in its heat. Close to the surface of the animal the heat would have gone in and out through the skin, especially on the narrow parts like the neck and the tail—as it does on this lizard basking in the Sun. But in the depths of the great body the temperature would have remained the same. In the same way, water in a big kettle may still feel warm an hour after it has boiled, but the same water in a small cup cools very quickly.

DINOSAUR SENSES

▽ In the dusk, the meat-eater *Troodon* snaps at a passing dragonfly.

We guess it could do this because the size of its brain shows that it could react quickly, and the position of its eyes means that it could focus on fast-moving prey. The big eye sockets suggest that this dinosaur was active at twilight, like an owl.

We see with our eyes, we smell with our noses, we hear through our ears, we taste with our tongues, and we feel things through the nerves in our skins. These are our senses, and with them we find out what the world around us is like. It is the same for most other animals. It would have been the same for the dinosaurs, too.

Different animals have keener senses as needed for survival. For example, dogs have a better sense of smell than we have, but we have better eyesight than rhinoceroses. It is difficult to tell how well dinosaurs' senses worked, since eyes, tongues, and other soft body parts do not fossilize. The skulls of some hunting dinosaurs, like *Troodon,* have enormous eye sockets, and so we can tell that these animals had big eyes. The position of the eyes means that they could focus both of them on the same object and therefore judge distances easily and well. Most plant-eating dinosaurs, such as *Hypsilophodon,* had eyes at the sides of their heads. This would have given them an all-round view so that they could see danger coming from any direction.

The size of the nostrils similarly can tell us about smell. Some long-necked plant-eaters, for instance *Brachiosaurus,* had enormous nostrils and so they probably had a good sense of smell. The meat-eaters like *Tyrannosaurus,* on the other hand, had very small nostrils. They probably did not hunt by smell as modern wolves do, but relied more on sight.

Separate parts of the brain control different functions. We can tell what a dinosaur's brain could do by taking a cast of the space it filled in the skull. If we find that the area for the sense of hearing is well developed compared with that for sight, then in life the animal would have relied on sound rather than vision.

Hunting eyesight
Present-day hunting birds like this owl have eyes that focus forward on their prey. Each eye forms a slightly different image of an object, and the brain can use this information to work out the object's distance. This is referred to as stereoscopic vision, and many of the hunting dinosaurs, such as *Troodon*, had it. However, like owls, it was limited to an area directly in front of them. To see all around, they had to turn their heads from side to side.

DINOSAUR SKIN

Dinosaur skin is not preserved. Occasionally, though, where a dinosaur's dead body has been buried quickly before the skin rots, an impression, or mark, of the skin surface is left in the rocks. The impressions show that many dinosaurs had skin covered with scales. These were not overlapping scales, like those of most modern lizards, but tiny, horny lumps that lay close to one another forming a jigsawlike pattern. Some dinosaurs had bigger horny plates embedded in the skin, and these were often preserved with the skeleton.

Although there is some evidence for the texture, or feel, of dinosaur skin, the color of this skin is pure guesswork. In one book you may see *Stegosaurus* with a green body with brown patches, and red and yellow plates. In another book, *Stegosaurus* will be brown above and yellow beneath, with blue plates. This just reflects different people's ideas about dinosaur color.

We can look at the colors in modern animals and see how each animal's color is related to its behavior. Hunting animals, like tigers and leopards, are often striped or spotted. Animals of open country, such as antelopes, may be countershaded, having dark colors on top and light colors beneath.

◁ A peacock shows a colorful display of feathers to attract a peahen. We know that the dinosaurs had good eyesight and would have been able to react to such displays. Maybe dinosaurs had similar bright signaling devices, like colorful crests, horns, or eyespots on the ends of their tails.

Club at end of tail

Dull colors
Plant-eaters that were not aggressive, like *Bactrosaurus*, were probably drably colored with greens and browns in order to blend in with their surroundings so that meat-eaters would not see them.

Bactrosaurus

Pentaceratops

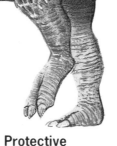

The youngsters of woodland animals like deer often have fur with patches of color. These are all types of camouflage, or ways of blending in with the surroundings to be difficult to see. Very big animals like elephants, which neither hunt nor have great enemies, do not need camouflage and so are an even gray color. These color schemes may also have applied to the dinosaurs in their various lifestyles.

Generally, dinosaurs were probably more colorful than modern mammals since they had better color vision. They may have used their bright colors for display or as a warning.

Protective
The horned-face dinosaurs, like *Pentaceratops* and *Triceratops,* had a bony frill protecting the neck. The armored ankylosaurs had skin on the back studded with bony knobs and studs and covered with horn. Ankylosaurs are often preserved upside-down in rocks formed in ancient rivers.

The weight of the armored skin on the back turned the dead animal over in the water.

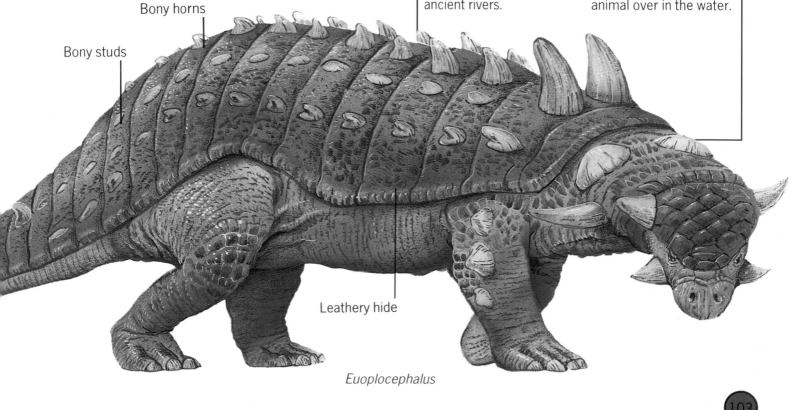

Bony horns

Bony studs

Leathery hide

Euoplocephalus

COMMUNICATION

Animals communicate with one another. They may not use words and sentences as we do, but they can make themselves sufficiently well understood for their ways of life. They can do it by visual signals, like a peacock using its tail or certain types of lizards using their brightly colored throat flaps. The dinosaurs could probably exchange all sorts of information in this way. Animals can also communicate by smell, like a skunk secreting a smelly liquid. We do not know if dinosaurs could communicate like this, but some did have very big nostrils, which makes us believe they had a good sense of smell.

Probably the best way of communicating over a great distance is by using sound. If you have heard a cat howling at night or a guard dog barking, you know how effective this can be. Wolves hunting in a pack call to one another so that every member of the pack knows where all the others are. That way, they can work together to ambush prey.

It is difficult to tell if the dinosaurs could make noises. Most animal noises are made by the lungs, the throat, and the vocal cords, which are soft structures that do not fossilize. However, the casts of various dinosaur brains show us that dinosaurs had good hearing. The skulls of the two-footed plant-eater *Corythosaurus* have been found with the delicate ear bones still intact. These show that this dinosaur at least could hear very well.

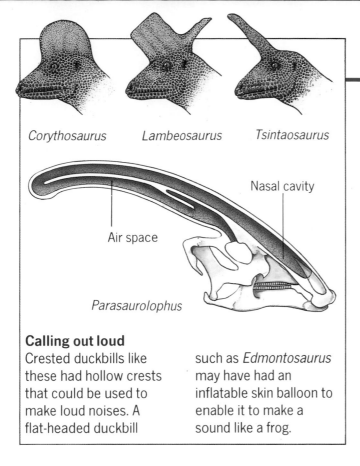

Corythosaurus   Lambeosaurus   Tsintaosaurus

Nasal cavity

Air space

Parasaurolophus

Calling out loud

Crested duckbills like these had hollow crests that could be used to make loud noises. A flat-headed duckbill such as *Edmontosaurus* may have had an inflatable skin balloon to enable it to make a sound like a frog.

Corythosaurus belonged to a group of dinosaurs called the duckbills. These all had a strangely shaped head with a ducklike beak. Some types had a very flattened head, and some had an extravagant crest. The crests were formed from the nose bones and were full of channels that the air from the nostrils had to pass through before reaching the lungs. They were probably used as sounding tubes for making noises, rather like the curved and twisted tubes of musical instruments such as the trumpet and saxophone. The crested duckbills could probably communicate with one another using toots and blares that would echo through the forests.

▷ The howler monkey of South and Central America has a very loud voice. Using a voice box in its throat, it can make a noise that can be heard for almost half a mile through the rainforests. Dinosaurs may have been able to communicate with one another by making similar kinds of sounds.

◁ A herd of the duckbilled dinosaurs, *Parasaurolophus*, and another duckbill, a *Brachylophosaurus*, browse at the edge of the forest. The herd is spread out, with some individuals out of sight. As a big meat-eater appears, the closest *Parasaurolophus* makes a noise like a horn, and all the duckbills get on their guard.

EGG LAYING

Reptiles lay eggs. It was always assumed that dinosaurs did so, too. But the first proof of this came in the 1920s when an American expedition to Mongolia found the remains of dinosaurs.

As well as the dinosaurs themselves, the scientists found the remains of their nests and, in them, eggs. The dinosaurs concerned were all of a small, horned species, *Protoceratops*. In life, it would have been about the size of a present-day sheep. The eggs were oval-shaped, about 3 inches across and almost 6 inches long. There were up to 30 of them, arranged in the nest in a spiral with their pointed ends inwards. The nest would have been a hollow in the sand, for it had been a sandy place where *Protoceratops* lived. Several females seemed to have laid their eggs in the same nest. By chance, found at one of the nests was the fossil skeleton of the egg-eating dinosaur *Oviraptor*. It seems that this animal had been overwhelmed by a sandstorm while it was raiding the nest.

The eggs of a 40-foot-long dinosaur
Since then the eggs of several other kinds of dinosaurs have been found. The largest dinosaur eggs known belong to one of the long-necked plant-eaters, *Hypselosaurus*. The eggs were found in France. These were not laid in nests but in pairs in a line. It is as if the mother dinosaur had laid them while walking. These eggs are about 10 inches in diameter, not much larger than those of an ostrich. Yet the adult dinosaur would have been much bigger than an ostrich. In fact, a hard-shelled egg like that of a bird could not have been any larger without a thicker shell to support it. And a thicker shell would have made it more difficult for the baby dinosaur to break out.

Inside the egg
A dinosaur's egg, like a modern reptile's, contained the baby animal and a yolk—its food supply. The whole thing was protected by a leathery shell. The baby dinosaur hatched when it was able to live in the open air.

Embryo

Yolk food supply

Shell

Protective membrane

Dinosaur eggs

△ The Nile crocodile, a modern reptile, nests in groups in special nesting grounds, as here. The mothers bury their eggs in the sand to keep them warm and wait for their young to hatch out. The large number of animals nesting in the same place threatens any predators that may want to eat the eggs or the young. Dinosaurs seem to have nested in a similar way.

◁ A lone mother *Protoceratops* rests by her newly laid eggs and watches over them. As with some modern reptiles, a few dinosaurs may have given birth to live young.

FAMILY LIFE

Adult birds usually look after their young until they are old enough to leave the nest and look after themselves. It seems that dinosaurs did the same.

In Montana in the United States, in the 1970s, scientists found the remains of a complete dinosaur nesting site. The nests were made by a type of two-footed plant-eater, a duckbill species called *Maiasaura* that lived in herds. Each nest would have been about 6 feet in diameter and 30 inches high. It would have been a mound of soil with a hollow at the top 30 inches deep. The nests were spaced about one dinosaur length (about 30 feet) apart. In them were eggs, baby dinosaurs, and, most importantly, youngsters, which were about 3 feet long.

◁ Beneath a bed of twigs and leaves in a *Maiasaura* nest, the young dinosaurs hatch out. A nestful of hatchling *Maiasaura* is a wriggling mass of squawking noise. At about 12 inches long, each baby is far too small and weak to look after itself. It may have had a little horn on the nose, which would later have been lost. The baby used the horn to break out of its egg. For the first few months of their lives, the youngsters would have been fed, protected and looked after in the nest by the adults.

The young dinosaurs had teeth that were worn from feeding, but their limb bones were too weak to have allowed them to go looking for food. This shows that the youngsters must have stayed in the nest until they were partly grown. They must have been looked after by the adults during this growing-up period.

We can imagine this nesting site as being like that of the flamingo. The young creatures live in the nests while their parents go off and find food for them. Any meat-eating animal that approaches is chased off by the parents that are still on the site.

The young dinosaurs probably remained in the nest for a few months, occasionally being led out by a parent to learn to find food for themselves. These trips would have become longer and longer, and eventually the youngsters would have been mature enough to join the herd and migrate with them.

Feeding young chicks
Birds, the modern relatives of the dinosaurs, have young that must be looked after carefully. Here, an adult song thrush feeds her young in a nest built in the branches of a pine tree. Birds make all kinds of nests, ranging from holes in the ground and piles of mud, to clumps of sticks in trees. We do not know of many fossil dinosaur nests. It may well be that there were several other types of dinosaur nests that we have not yet discovered.

SIZE AND LIFESPAN

The dinosaurs ranged from little chicken-sized creatures to giant animals more than 100 feet long. Their ways of life, growth rates, and lifespans were probably as varied as the dinosaurs themselves.

It is difficult to tell how old individual dinosaurs were when they died. We can look at some skeletons and see the kinds of damage, such as broken bones and fused joints, that the animals experienced during life. If the bones seem to have suffered a great deal of wear and tear, we can be fairly sure that their owners were very old individuals. Sometimes big bones have growth rings, like those of a tree trunk. Each ring shows the growth that took place in one year.

Chicken-sized
The smallest known dinosaur was the little meat-eating species, *Compsognathus*. It was about 35 inches long when fully grown, but most of this was neck and tail, and it weighed about 5 pounds. This would have made it the size of a small chicken. We know of dinosaur skeletons smaller than a chicken's, but these are all from babies.

Baby *Diplodocus*

Studies of dinosaur growth rings suggest that some of the biggest long-necked plant-eaters may have reached an age of 100 years before they died. Cold-blooded animals live longer than warm-blooded ones. If the long-necked plant-eaters were purely cold-blooded, they may have reached ages of 200 years or more. How fast dinosaurs grew is difficult to tell from fossil bones. Studies of the *Maiasaura* nests in Montana suggest that these two-footed plant-eaters were only about 12 inches long when they hatched, but after a year of being fed by their parents they were 15 feet long and big enough to leave the nest. They would have been fully grown—30 feet long—after three years.

Baby dinosaurs
The smallest dinosaur skeleton found was about the size of a blackbird's. It was called *Mussaurus*, or "mouse lizard." The skeleton lacked a tail and was only 8 inches long. It was a baby's skeleton.

We know this because it had eyes, head, and feet too large for its body size. These are the most developed parts of a baby dinosaur. The adult was perhaps a long-necked plant-eater about 10 feet long.

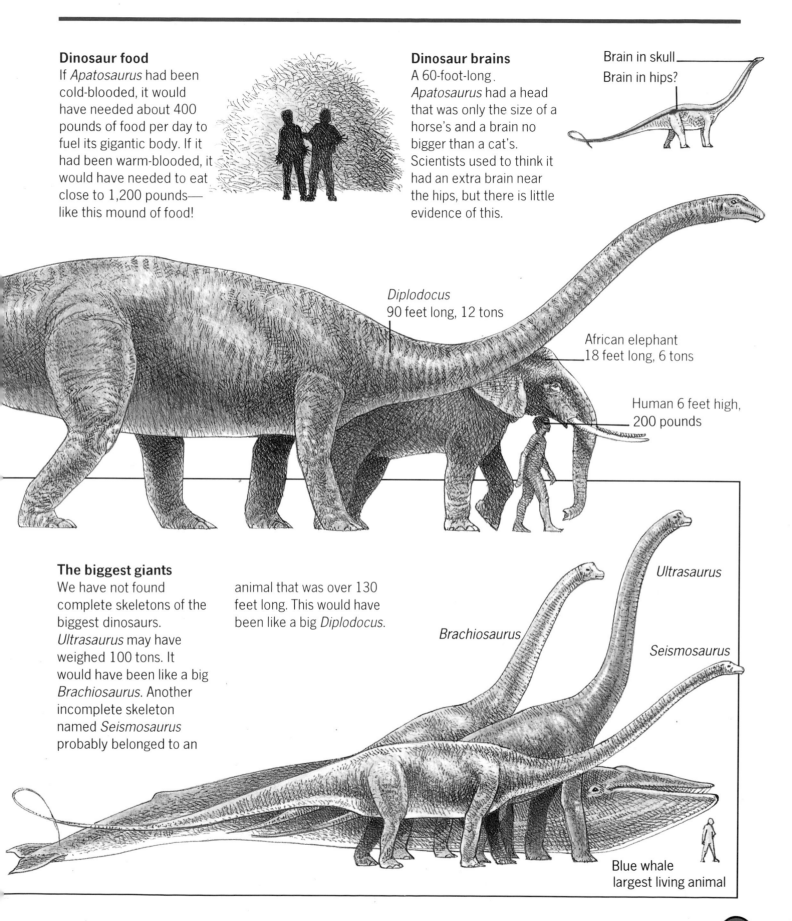

Dinosaur food
If *Apatosaurus* had been cold-blooded, it would have needed about 400 pounds of food per day to fuel its gigantic body. If it had been warm-blooded, it would have needed to eat close to 1,200 pounds—like this mound of food!

Dinosaur brains
A 60-foot-long. *Apatosaurus* had a head that was only the size of a horse's and a brain no bigger than a cat's. Scientists used to think it had an extra brain near the hips, but there is little evidence of this.

Brain in skull
Brain in hips?

Diplodocus
90 feet long, 12 tons

African elephant
18 feet long, 6 tons

Human 6 feet high,
200 pounds

The biggest giants
We have not found complete skeletons of the biggest dinosaurs. *Ultrasaurus* may have weighed 100 tons. It would have been like a big *Brachiosaurus*. Another incomplete skeleton named *Seismosaurus* probably belonged to an animal that was over 130 feet long. This would have been like a big *Diplodocus*.

Ultrasaurus

Brachiosaurus

Seismosaurus

Blue whale
largest living animal

GROUP LIVING

There are advantages to living in groups. The main one is safety. If there are a lot of you, an enemy will think twice before attacking. If you are attacked, the enemy may get your neighbor and not you. Dinosaurs may have moved about in big herds for just this reason.

The big, long-necked, plant-eaters seemed to have behaved in this way. In Texas there are fossil trackways made by these dinosaurs on the move that show the footprints of the smaller and younger animals in the middle of the herd, with the big ones on each side. Any meat-eater would have to break through a barrier of adult dinosaurs to try to reach a defenseless youngster.

It is possible that the horned dinosaurs also lived in herds. Their remains are often found in numbers large enough to suggest this. We have seen how adult females of the two-footed plant-eaters gathered in groups to lay their eggs. They may have stayed in their groups, along with their young, all their lives.

It was not just the plant-eaters that went about in groups. Some of the medium-sized hunters did so, too. Wolf-sized *Deinonychus* probably hunted in packs. In one dinosaur find in Montana, several *Deinonychus* skeletons were found in the same rock formation as bones of a two-footed plant-eater, *Tenontosaurus*. It may be that a pack of the meat-eaters was feasting on the plant-eater when they were all killed, perhaps by lightning. In such an attack, one hunter could have gone for the victim's head while the others tore at the flesh of its belly with their big claws.

▷ A small herd of *Styracosaurus* grazes quietly among the ferns on a sunny slope. Their peace is suddenly shattered by a big *Albertosaurus* that bursts forward from the nearby forest, hissing loudly, intent on killing one of the young. At the approach of the enemy the herd bunches together so that the huge horns of the adults are pointing outward to form a barrier and defensive wall.

Living as a herd
In the modern world, the musk oxen of Greenland and northern Canada live as a herd. They often bunch together, either to keep warm or for safety reasons. Should a wolf pack attack the herd, the oxen all crowd together in a circle, as here, with the vulnerable females and the youngsters in the center. Usually the predators soon become discouraged and go off to find easier prey.

MIGRATION

The horned dinosaur *Pachyrhinosaurus* used to be known from only two skulls. Then in 1985, more skeletons of this animal were discovered in one place in Alberta, Canada—more than a thousand skeletons, in fact! In this great mass of bone were the remains of babies, of partly grown individuals, and of fully grown adults. A whole herd of these dinosaurs had suddenly died in one location. There were actually too many *Pachyrhinosaurus* remains in this bone bed.

At that place all those millions of years ago there would not have been enough food for a population as big as that. The most likely explanation is that the herd was migrating from one feeding ground to another and was crossing a river when a sudden flood caught the animals by surprise and drowned them.

Such events happen nowadays when huge herds of migrating animals—for example, wildebeest or caribou—have to cross rivers in their path. Many can be washed away and killed by sudden flash floods. In 1984 about 4,000 caribou perished when they were trying to cross a flooded river in Quebec, Canada.

Moving as conditions change
The bone bed in Alberta dates from near the end of the Age of Dinosaurs. At that time, the continents, the huge landmasses of the world, had broken up and were drifting apart. Each continent would have had its own cycle of seasons, from winter to summer or dry season to rainy, and the dinosaur herds would have journeyed from one place to another at certain times of the year. Another bed of this period, but in Texas, shows footprints of many long-necked plant-eaters heading south. Some scientists see this, too, as evidence of dinosaur migration.

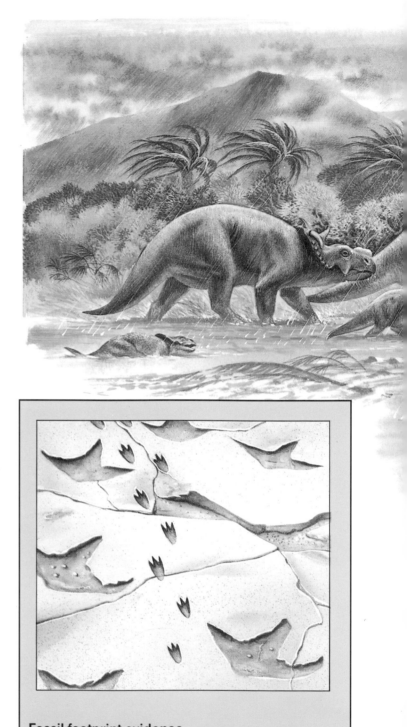

Fossil footprint evidence
Footprints of dinosaur herds are known from the whole Age of Dinosaurs. In many cases the footprints are all heading in one direction, as though the herd had been moving for a particular reason —for instance, to find new feeding grounds or avoid cold weather.

△ A small herd of *Pachyrhinosaurus* crosses an old river course in a storm. The animals are unaware that rain in the hills is about to produce a flood that will gush down the river channel and drown them. The sudden death of many animals left masses of fossil bones, which we find as bone beds.

▷ In modern times, as the dry season starts in Tanzania, East Africa, huge herds of wildebeest migrate in search of grass to eat. Many wildebeest drown or die from injuries as they try to cross rivers.

EXTINCTION

We do not really know how the dinosaurs became extinct, or died out. What we do know is that after 160 million years of success, the dinosaurs suddenly disappeared about 65 million years ago, never to be seen again.

Their disappearance could have been fairly quick, or it could have been quite slow, lasting a few million years. It is difficult to tell from the rocks laid down at the time. Many different theories have been put forward to explain their disappearance. One of the most popular theories now is that the Earth was struck by a giant meteorite or a swarm of comets at that time, causing serious changes to the climate.

Meteorite strike
The impact of a meteorite six miles across would have pierced the Earth's crust and blasted molten rock, ash, and dust into the atmosphere.

Hot, then cool
Some scientists think that the climates cooled naturally at the end of the Age of Dinosaurs. One effect of this may have been that dinosaur babies of only one sex were born, as can happen in crocodiles and turtles today. As a result, they would not have been able to breed and would have died out within only one or two generations.

Changing seas
Toward the end of the Age of Dinosaurs, the area of sea became less than it had been for a long time. This would have led to a change in climate in which the air temperature would have risen by several degrees. The dinosaurs' body temperature-regulating systems might not have been able to cope with this.

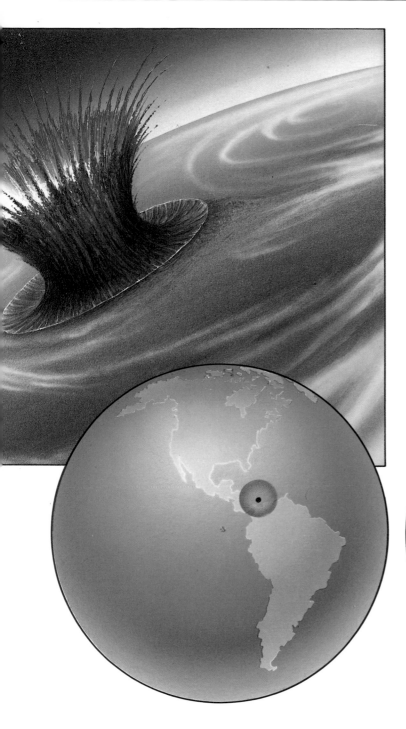

A meteorite strike would have sent up clouds of steam and dust into the atmosphere, blocking out the Sun's warmth for months. The vegetation would have died back and the plant-eating dinosaurs would have starved. With no prey to feed upon, the meat-eaters would also have starved. When the skies cleared, the vegetation would have grown back, but it would have been too late for the dinosaurs. Less dramatic explanations involve the steady change of the climates and the vegetation, or changes brought about by the movements of the continents. The dinosaurs may not have been able to evolve quickly enough to keep up with these changes.

Cool, then hot
There is evidence for a meteorite strike 65 million years ago near present-day Central America. After the impact, the cloud of dust would have blocked out sunlight, cooling the Earth. Once the dust had settled, the steam left in the atmosphere would then have produced a "greenhouse effect," heating the planet.

After the dinosaurs
Whatever happened 65 million years ago, it wiped out many other animal groups as well. But some of the mammals and birds survived, and it was these that then evolved and developed to take the place of the great reptiles. Soon the Earth was alive again, and the dinosaurs no more than a memory.

The Age of Dinosaurs

The first dinosaurs appeared about 225 million years ago (mya for short) in what scientists call the Late Triassic Period. They thrived through the following Jurassic Period and died out at the end of the Cretaceous Period 65 million years ago. During this time, geography, climate, and vegetation, or plant life, were constantly changing—as shown in these dinosaur scenes.

Triassic 245–208 mya
A single giant landmass or supercontinent, mostly desert conditions, tree ferns, and conifers.

Early and Middle Jurassic 208–157 mya Supercontinent, shallow seas, moist climate, tree ferns, conifers, and cycads.

FIVE

The Fossil Hunters

When the first dinosaur bones were found, no one could explain them. They were thought to be the bones of giants, or of sinners that were killed in the great flood of the Book of Genesis in the Bible. Only in the nineteenth century did people begin to look at these fossils scientifically. They found them to be the remains of giant reptiles that walked the Earth millions of years before people existed. At first these animals were considered to be like giant lizards. As more and more remains were found, it became clearer what kinds of animals these were.

Today we have more information so that we believe we know all about these great creatures and the other living things of the past. But every year brings new discoveries. As new information is gathered, scientists come up with new theories about prehistoric life. The excitement of the study of fossil remains—a science we call paleontology—is that our views are constantly changing and need updating. Our knowledge of the past continually develops as we move into the future. And although the dinosaurs are long dead, our picture of them is still evolving.

Late Jurassic 157–146 mya
Supercontinent beginning to break up, dry inland, moist climates by coasts.

Early Cretaceous 146–97 mya
Continents drifting into separate landmasses, plant life as in Triassic and Jurassic periods.

Late Cretaceous 97–65 mya
Separate continents, each with its own animal life, and plants like modern types.

CATASTROPHE

About 140 million years ago, a broad lake lay across much of northwest Europe. To the north of it, ridges of rock stretched from Wales to Belgium. The English Channel did not exist then. Streams cut ravines through the ridges, forming steep slopes of limestone, sandstone, and coal laid down nearly 200 million years earlier. The streams flowed southward toward the lake. At the edge of the lake they spread out to form deltas—fan-shaped, muddy, swampy areas. The ravines, slopes, and deltas were covered in forests of conifer trees. Ferns and cycads grew beneath the conifers, forming a thick undergrowth. Horsetails grew along the banks of the lake.

This was the landscape of the dinosaurs. Along the lake's edge and in the swamps roamed herds of the two-footed plant-eater *Iguanodon,* and its small, fast-moving relative *Hypsilophodon*. Big meat-eaters such as *Baryonyx* hunted through the undergrowth. In the skies flew pterosaurs. Crocodiles and turtles wallowed in the shallow water. It was a lush landscape in which many creatures lived. Many died there as well.

Among the ravines of one of the ridges there was a depression, a giant hollow in the ground. This was frequently washed by flash floods following rainstorms. During one such flood, an *Iguanodon* was caught and drowned by the waters while crossing the river farther up, and its dead body was washed into the depression. Then another dead *Iguanodon* was washed down, and its body settled beside the first. Eventually so many dead bodies of *Iguanodon* had gathered that the hollow became a true dinosaurs' graveyard.

▷ An *Iguanodon* is carried down a gorge by a flash flood as other *Iguanodon* look on. It settles in a hollow. Minutes earlier, the *Iguanodon* was grazing on the river bank. This was the first part of the process that turned the dinosaur into remains preserved in rock—into fossils—that we can see today.

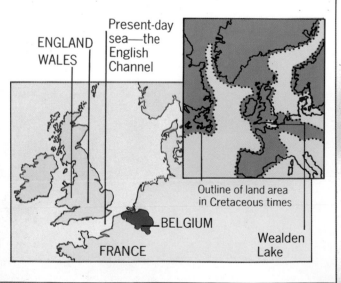

Location of the graveyard
In the Early Cretaceous Period, northern North America was joined to Europe, and a sea called the Tethys separated Europe and Africa. On the northern European continent there was a warm shallow lake called the Wealden, as on this map. Along the forested shores of this lake roamed dinosaurs like *Iguanodon*.

ENGLAND WALES

Present-day sea—the English Channel

Outline of land area in Cretaceous times

BELGIUM

FRANCE

Wealden Lake

TIME PASSES

Within a few weeks, the soft parts of the dead bodies of the *Iguanodon*—skin, muscles, hearts, brains, stomachs, lungs, and so on—rotted away. But the hard parts, the bones, did not. They stayed unchanged and still joined together as skeletons. The dead bodies of other animals lying out on open ground had been torn to bits by scavenging animals, and their bones were now broken and scattered. In the hollow, the bones of the *Iguanodon* had not been disturbed. But they had become covered by layers of mud, sand, and soil laid on top of them by the river.

Over many thousands of years the landscape changed. The river wore deeper into the ridge. The ridge itself became worn down by wind, rain, and ice. Sediment built up in the bottom of the gorge, and the river no longer washed down dead bodies. The mud and sand that had settled over the bones of the *Iguanodon* started to turn them to rock. Water trickling and seeping through the ground filled empty spaces in the bones with minerals. These included silica and iron pyrite. (Silica is the main mineral of sand, and iron pyrite is a kind of iron ore.) This replacement of living matter with minerals is called fossilization. It caused the shapes of the *Iguanodon* bones to be preserved for all time.

With other dinosaurs, their bones rotted away only after the sediment had turned to rock. They left holes in the rock called molds. These filled up with minerals from rainwater and formed lumps in the shapes of the original bones. The lumps are known as casts. A few dinosaur fossils contained nothing of the original creatures—just their footprints where they had walked in mud.

▽ *Iguanodon* bodies washed down from the surrounding hills formed a dinosaur graveyard that was to remain hidden for millions of years.

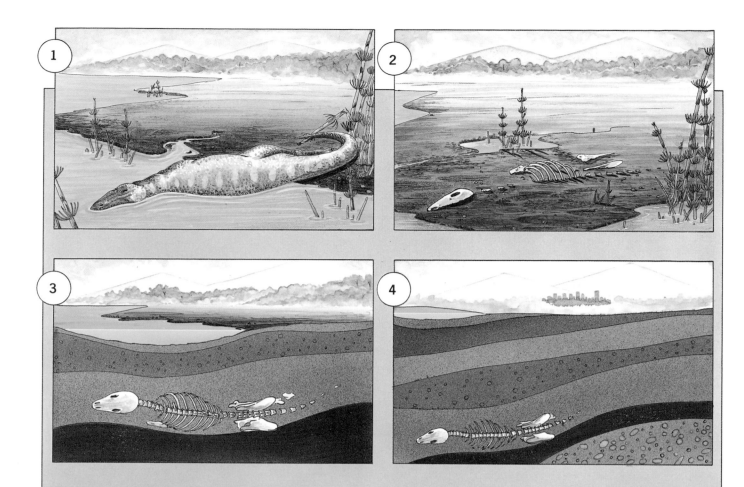

Turning dinosaurs into rocks

The body of a dead *Iguanodon* settles on the bottom of a river (1). It is buried by the mud and sand washed down, and its flesh rots away (2). Eventually other layers of sediment pile up above it. Forces and pressures within the crust, the skin of the Earth, turn these layers into beds of rock, and the bones are filled with minerals (3). Now the fossil skeleton lies hidden in the rocks below our feet (4). The whole process of fossilization takes millions of years. Rock that is made up almost entirely of fossil bones is called a bone bed.

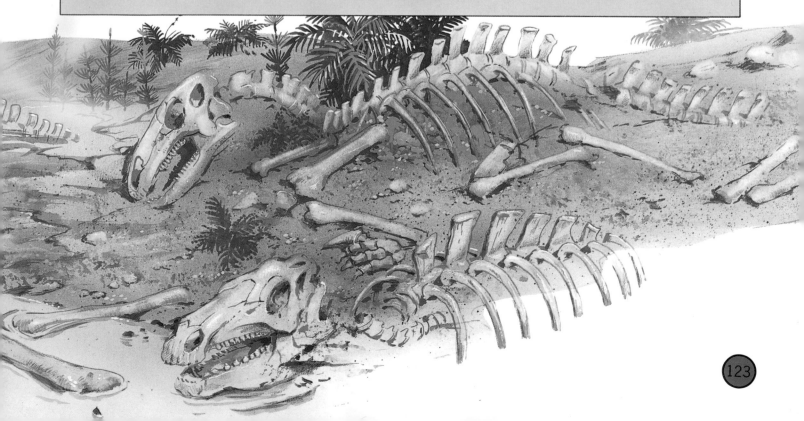

THE CHANGING LAND

It has been 140 million years since the *Iguanodon* bodies were deposited and buried. The ridge of rocks with the *Iguanodon* graveyard in the gorge was worn down by the weather, and a sea of warm water spread over the whole area for a while. The continents were continuing to move, and Africa began to push against Europe. In northern Europe this movement raised the land, and the shallow sea drained away. Forests grew everywhere, but as the climate gradually changed, these gave way to grasslands. By this time North America had broken away from Europe and the Atlantic Ocean had formed between them. Finally, in the last 2 million years or so, the landscape became as it is today.

While this had been happening, the animal life had changed. The dinosaurs had died out and the mammals had taken their place.

The first finds and early fossil hunters

This painting shows fossil hunters at a chalk pit in Cambridgeshire, southern England, in 1822.
With the discovery of *Megalosaurus*, *Iguanodon*, and fossils of other similar animals, scientists began to realize that a whole group of giant reptiles once walked the Earth. In 1842, British scientist Sir Richard Owen gave this group the name *Dinosauria*, meaning "terrible lizards."

About 250,000 years ago, one particular species of mammal, the first humans, moved into the area. As people began to explore their surroundings, they tried to make sense of the natural world. They developed ideas about how rocks were formed, and how the shells and bones of living things of the past were turned to stone and embedded in them.

The first recognizable dinosaur bones were discovered in southern England early in the nineteenth century. The first dinosaur to be described and named was *Megalosaurus,* meaning great lizard. This was a big meat-eater. William Buckland, a scientist at Oxford University, did this work in 1824 based on a single fossil jawbone with teeth. The second dinosaur to be discovered was *Iguanodon* in 1825. But this, too, was in England, not in Belgium at the *Iguanodon* graveyard.

◁ The small town of Bernissart in southwest Belgium in the 1870s. This cutaway view of the coal mine below ground shows elevator shafts and passages cut by miners through the layers of rock in order to reach and to dig out the coal. There are also objects buried in the rocks—the *Iguanodon* fossils or remains. Above ground are the mine buildings.

◁ The first *Iguanodon* remains were found in southern England. In 1825, Gideon Mantell, an English country doctor, gave the animals the name *Iguanodon*, meaning "iguana tooth," because he thought that their teeth looked like those of the modern iguana lizard. He made this drawing of the whole animal based on these remains.

AWAITING DISCOVERY

The idea of dinosaurs became very popular in nineteenth-century Europe. The work of fossil hunters William Buckland on *Megalosaurus* and Gideon Mantell on *Iguanodon* caught the imagination of the public. In natural history books made at the time, illustrations of both these dinosaurs, shown as giant lizards, were often included. So, too, were illustrations of fossil sea reptiles, like the long-necked plesiosaurs and the fish-shaped ichthyosaurs. These extinct creatures had been known for a number of years.

In 1851 the Great Exhibition of the Works of Industry of All Nations was held in Hyde Park in London. The main exhibition hall was a huge structure of steel, glass, and wood called the Crystal Palace. After the exhibition closed, the Crystal Palace was taken apart and put up again in a park in Sydenham, south London. The park was renamed Crystal Palace.

The first dinosaur theme park
In Crystal Palace Park in south London stand these concrete dinosaur statues. They were built in 1854 with instructions from English fossil hunter Sir Richard Owen. We now know that the animals did not look like this, but they were good models considering the little information on dinosaurs available at the time.

Miners discover strange shapes in the coal seam.

More evidence, new interpretations

In the grounds of Crystal Palace were placed full-sized statues of the dinosaurs and other fossil animals as they were known at the time. The Crystal Palace itself is long gone—destroyed in a fire in 1936—but the beautiful dinosaur statues are still there.

The idea that dinosaurs were lizards built like elephants remained for some time. Then, in 1858, part of a dinosaur skeleton was found in New Jersey in the United States. It was studied by Joseph Leidy, professor of anatomy at the University of Pennsylvania, and he named it *Hadrosaurus,* meaning "thick lizard." It was similar to *Iguanodon,* but there was enough of the skeleton to show that in life it had not resembled an elephant-like lizard. Instead, it must have looked more like a kangaroo, standing on its long hind legs with its shorter front legs dangling before it.

In 1868, Benjamin Waterhouse Hawkins, the sculptor who had created the Crystal Palace statues, mounted the *Hadrosaurus* skeleton for Leidy at the Academy of Natural Sciences in Philadelphia, Pennsylvania—the first mounted dinosaur skeleton ever exhibited.

Shortly afterwards, in 1878, coal miners in Bernissart, Belgium, were tunneling through a coal seam when the coal suddenly gave out. Instead of coal they found clay filled with strange-looking lumps. The *Iguanodon* graveyard had been discovered.

△ A reconstruction of an *Iguanodon* found on the Isle of Wight, England, in 1917. It is one of the most complete dinosaur skeletons found in the British Isles.

FINISHING THE PUZZLE

The Belgian coal miner Jules Creteur, who found the oddly shaped lumps in the mine at Bernissart, brought them to the surface and examined them. He found that they were bits of fossilized bone. Creteur had been tunneling through the rocks of the ancient ridge and had discovered the depression filled with Cretaceous sediments and the *Iguanodon* graveyard.

Mining work was stopped. A team from the Royal Museum of Natural History in Brussels was brought in, and experts began to dig out the skeletons. In three years, thirty-nine *Iguanodon* skeletons were brought up to the surface of the mine. These were mostly complete, unlike the earlier *Iguanodon* finds of Mantell and others in England.

The scientist best known for the dinosaur work done at Bernissart is Louis Dollo of the Royal Museum of Natural History, Brussels. In 1882 he began to study and reconstruct the skeletons. In Brussels, in a building that was once a chapel, he and his team mounted eleven of the most complete skeletons in lifelike poses—a job that took 30 years. Dollo believed that *Iguanodon* probably moved about on its hind legs, unlike the modern iguana. The Belgian king of the time, Leopold II, visited the display and remarked

The fossil *Iguandon* embedded in the rock.

that the *Iguanodon* looked like giraffes, with their tall necks and small heads. In any case, the skeletons suggested an animal that was very different from the elephant-like lizards drawn by Mantell.

Dollo found that there were two different sizes of *Iguanodon*. He thought these may have represented two different species or types, or the males and females of just one species. We now believe that the first explanation was correct: there are several *Iguanodon* species.

▽ Once the skeletons were in Brussels, one of the researchers, G. Lavalette, made these drawings in the positions in which they were buried.

▽ The complete *Iguanodon* skeletons were too large to be moved in single pieces. Mine workers and scientists sawed them up into blocks, then numbered the blocks, removed them from the ground, and put them back together in order in the laboratory.

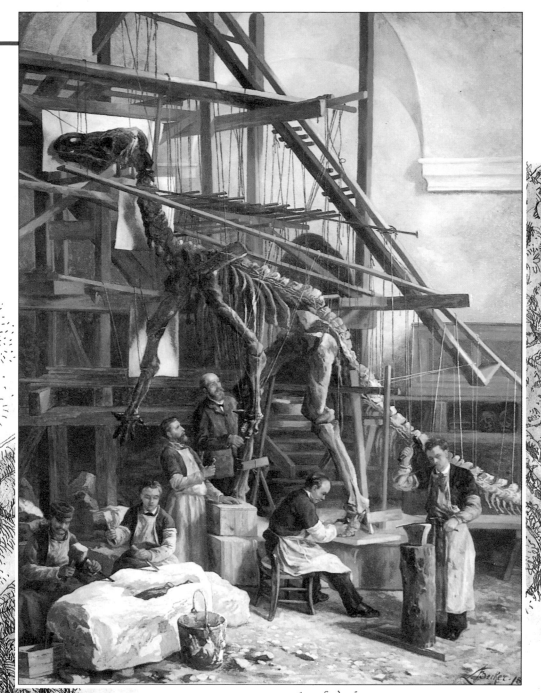

△ This painting, made from a photograph taken in 1889 by L. Becker, shows the first of the *Iguanodon* skeletons being put together in St. George's Chapel in Brussels. Even in its incomplete state, the animal's small head, massive tail, and the shape of its limbs, were obvious.

DINOSAUR FEVER

While studies of *Iguanodon* were being carried out in Europe, the attention of many fossil hunters switched to North America, where many dinosaur finds were being made.

In 1877 a British fossil collector, Arthur Lakes, and a naval captain from Connecticut, H.C. Beckwith, found some big bones at the foot of the Rocky Mountains at Morrison, near Denver, Colorado. Lakes sent a message to Othniel Charles Marsh, professor of paleontology at Yale University, asking for help. Marsh was slow to reply, so Lakes sent a similar message to the wealthy scientist and fossil collector Edward Drinker Cope in Philadelphia, Pennsylvania.

This sparked what were to become known as the Bone Wars. Cope and Marsh did not like one another. When Marsh realized that his rival and a team of paleontologists were at Morrison, he sent out his own team to make new dinosaur discoveries. Both men realized that the site, which geologists call the Morrison Formation, was going to be rich in fossils. Both Cope and Marsh hired workers armed with guns and rifles, and each poached the other's men and their fossil finds. It is said that one team would take what they wanted from an area and smash up everything else so that the other team would not get it. Most of the fighting centered on a hill called Como Bluff in Wyoming. There, huge numbers of dinosaur fossils could be seen at the surface.

During the Bone Wars many dinosaur fossils may have been destroyed, but the wars did do some good. Both Cope and Marsh wanted to get their finds shown in museums as quickly as possible, so they developed a way of uncovering the bones without damaging them. They left each bone partly buried in the rock and covered it with plaster of Paris. Then they cut out a block of rock with the bone still in it. The bone was removed from the rock in a laboratory, where it was easier to work. This technique is still used today. By the late 1890s, many new dinosaurs had been discovered. Marsh had found, among others, *Stegosaurus* and *Allosaurus,* while Cope had found *Camarasaurus* and *Coelophysis.*

The dinosaur hunters
Edward Drinker Cope and Othniel Charles Marsh used their own money to pay for dinosaur expeditions. Later, rich businessmen, such as the Scottish-born American Andrew Carnegie, paid for the hunting, study, and display in museums of dinosaur skeletons. Paleontologists named *Diplodocus carnegii* after him, and *Apatosaurus louisae* after his wife.

Edward Cope

Othniel Marsh

Andrew Carnegie

△ (Top) Dressed and armed for the dinosaur hunt, Marsh—center of back row—and his men pose for the camera.

△ Arthur Lakes was not only a fossil hunter but also an artist. He painted this picture of Marsh's men at work at Como Bluff.

FINDING DINOSAURS

Exposed by science
Dinosaur skeletons are usually found by members of scientific expeditions who know in what types and ages of rocks to look for them.

Uncovered in deserts
The dry desert winds wear away the surface of rocks. The fossils of dinosaur footprints in the rocks are eventually exposed.

Washed out by rivers
A river wearing away a hillside will expose the different rock layers, or strata, of which the hill is made. Fossils in the strata will be uncovered.

Since the days of Cope and Marsh, the hunt for dinosaurs has spread to all the continents. In the early years of this century, many discoveries were made in Canada, particularly in Alberta. This work was pioneered by the American fossil hunter Barnum Brown and followed by C.H. Sternberg and his three sons. The skeletons they found filled museums in New York, Ottawa, and Toronto.

Then Africa became the center for dinosaur discoveries. Between 1909 and 1929, in what is now Tanzania, German and British expeditions found dinosaurs like those of the Morrison Formation. In the 1920s, American expeditions to Mongolia found several fossil dinosaurs, including the first dinosaur eggs. In the 1970s and 1980s, spectacular dinosaur discoveries came from Mongolia, China, and South America. Recent finds have been in the United States, Canada, England, Greenland, Australia, and Antarctica.

DINOSAURS ALL AROUND THE WORLD
Dinosaur remains have been found on all continents.

- Triassic fossils
- Early and Middle Jurassic fossils
- Late Jurassic fossils
- Early Cretaceous fossils
- Late Cretaceous fossils

Exposed by the weather
Soft clays are easily washed away by rain. As they are removed, hard fossils in the clay, such as dinosaur bones, are left on the ground where they are preserved.

Found by chance
People walking along a riverbank or digging in a field may come across fossil bones. Usually they will report their finds to the local university or a museum, which will remove the bones for further studies.

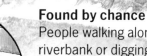

Europe

Asia

Africa

Australia

Antarctica

Today, paleontologists may set out to explore remote places where dinosaur bones are known to be common. These fossil hunts can be as dramatic as those in the days of Cope and Marsh. The most important part of such a trip is the preparation. A dinosaur-hunting expedition can cost tens of thousands of dollars. It may take many years to persuade governments and universities that it is money well spent and that they should pay for the trip. Politics may be a problem, too. Often the new dinosaur sites are situated in developing countries where there are civil wars or conflicts between neighboring peoples. These peoples are likely to be suspicious of foreigners digging around in their lands. In 1977, for instance, scientists on the International Paleontological Expedition to Nigeria spent Christmas in a Nigerian prison because the local people did not believe they were simply fossil hunting.

DIGGING UP THE PAST

Once a dinosaur skeleton has been found, a team of expert fossil hunters moves in. The team tries to find out the type of dinosaur the skeleton came from and how best to remove the bones from the ground.

At first, usually only part of the skeleton is seen. Perhaps someone finds a piece of bone at the foot of a slope and reports this discovery to a museum, which immediately sends a paleontologist to investigate. The paleontologist searches the cliffs above the slope to see from where the bone fragment fell. He finds more bones in a bed of rock exposed at the cliff-face. He concludes that the rest of the skeleton must lie deep within the rocks of the cliff.

Unearthing the skeleton

The fossil hunters use small bulldozers and excavators to clear away the rocks above the bed containing the skeleton. When they have dug down close to the skeleton, the earth-moving machines are taken away, and the rest of the rock material above the fossils is carefully cleared by hand. As each part of the skeleton is uncovered, it is measured, drawn, and photographed.

If the skeleton is buried in solid rock, the whole rock bed is cut up into large blocks, which are carried by truck to the museum. If the skeleton lies in soft material like clay, however, the team clears away the clay above the bones by hand. The exposed bones are

▽ Although fossil bones are made of mineral and have existed for hundreds of millions of years, they are very fragile. They must be protected by being filled with resin or coated with plaster of Paris or fiberglass, as here, before being transported to the museum.

◁ Once a fossil skeleton has been exposed, the first job is to get it under cover. It needs to be protected from the weather, which can break down some of the minerals in the fossils.

134

coated with wet paper and then with bandages or cloth soaked in plaster of Paris. When the top surface of each bone is completely coated and protected, the clay underneath is scraped away. The bone is then turned over, and the newly exposed side treated in the same way. The bone packages can then be carried off safely to the museum for the detailed work on the fossils.

Uncovering the bones

The paleontologists examine tiny fossils and structures in the rock itself as well as the bones, in order to build up a picture of the landscape in which the dinosaur lived.

Back at the museum, technicians known as preparators carefully remove the protective plaster cases or the rock containing the bones. They use power tools like dental drills for grinding or cutting away the rock. For delicate work, they use fine dental probes and even pins and sewing needles. Sometimes the preparators use chemicals to dissolve away the rock, or sound waves to shake the bones free. When their work is done the bones are ready for the paleontologists to study.

△▷ At the museum or laboratory, the protective casing is removed, as is any rock around the fossils. This process may take years, especially if acid has to be used to eat away the rock from around the bones. The acid is applied by brush or medicine dropper. Fossil preparation is very skilled, slow work.

THE BONES OF A DINOSAUR

If a dinosaur skeleton removed from rocks or the ground is almost complete, then the museum may decide to put it on display instead of keeping it in the laboratory for detailed study. (Only rarely are complete dinosaur skeletons found.)

Before any of this is done, however, the scientists must know the structure of the animal when it was alive—how its bones were joined together, how the joints moved, and whether it stood on two or four legs.

Making a dinosaur display is like building a skyscraper. A steel framework is built to support the skeleton. If the bones are too delicate to handle, a copy of the skeleton is made and this is displayed instead. First, a mold and cast are made of each bone. Then the casts are mounted, arranging them as a skeleton on the framework in a lifelike pose.

△ Sometimes, fossil dinosaur bones are so jumbled, like these of an *Iguanodon*, that they must be fitted together like a jigsaw puzzle to make a reconstruction.

The casts can be made with plaster, as in Andrew Carnegie's *Diplodocus* skeleton. He had ten copies made of all 300 bones, and gave the skeletons as gifts to museums around the world. Nowadays, though, more lightweight materials are used, such as hollow fiberglass. The Museum of Natural History in Denver, Colorado, has a 40-foot-long *Tyrannosaurus* skeleton that is so light it stands on one leg.

If a display dinosaur has any bones missing, casts of these are made from the bones of other skeletons of the same animal. Or a paleontologist makes casts based on what he or she thinks they may have looked like.

Tail of *Deinonychus* with interlocking bony bars

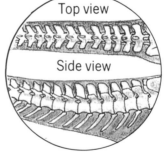

Top view

Side view

Bony bars

Side to side, or up and down? The tail of *Allosaurus* was tall and narrow. This suggests that it could move its tail from side to side more easily than it could move it up and down.

Flexible or stiff? The tail bones of some dinosaurs were surrounded by very long bony bars, making the tail rigid. This is not the case in *Allosaurus*.

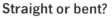

Straight or bent?
Allosaurus's knee joint showed that its hind legs were bent for most of the time.

How big a chest?
The size of the chest cavity gives clues about the size of the stomach, intestines, and lungs.

"Open wide"
The way the jawbones hang from the main part of the skull shows how the animal ate. Many meat-eaters had jaws that could expand sideways, allowing them to swallow huge chunks of meat.

▽ Many museums have spectacular mounted dinosaur skeletons on display. These are the skeletons of *Diplodocus*, left, and *Triceratops*, right, in the Central Hall of the Natural History Museum, London.

Skeleton of Allosaurus

FLESH ON THE BONES

The skeleton is only the starting point for restoring or making a copy of an extinct animal such as a dinosaur. It is just the supporting structure on which the living animal was built. The rest of the body, being made of soft tissues, never fossilized. The task of the scientist is to rebuild the complete animal from whatever clues and evidence he or she can find.

The first step is to put muscles on the bare bones. Here the bones themselves can provide some clues. In life the muscles were attached to the bones by tendons, and these sometimes left marks where they were connected to the bones. Next, a knowledge of engineering and construction is used. The scientist needs to understand what forces the dinosaur would have needed to move the various parts of its body. He or she needs to know how the bones could work as levers and pivots. From this the scientist can work out how the muscles would have been arranged to produce those forces.

With muscles over the bones, it is possible to get a good idea of the overall shape and size of the dinosaur. However, for a complete restoration, the scientist has to work out how parts of the body deep beneath the skin were laid out. This requires an understanding of

▷ Building up a complete picture of a dinosaur requires not only the making of a model or a mounted skeleton but also an understanding of the shape and structure of the dinosaur's body, how the animal lived, and how it behaved.

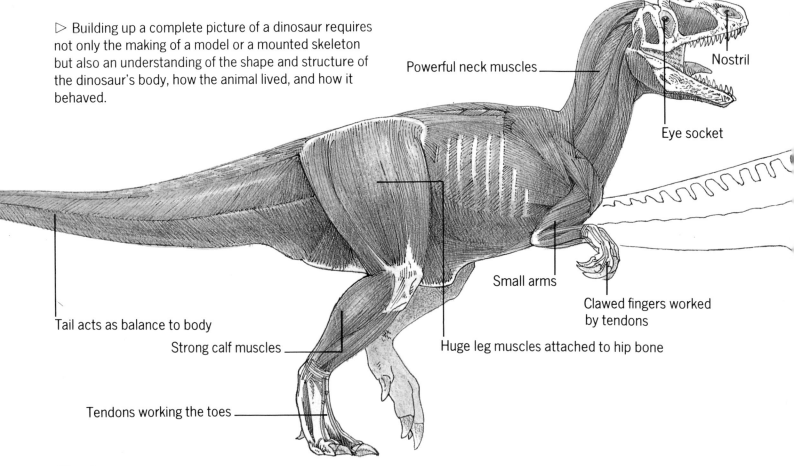

Powerful neck muscles

Nostril

Eye socket

Small arms

Clawed fingers worked by tendons

Tail acts as balance to body

Strong calf muscles

Huge leg muscles attached to hip bone

Tendons working the toes

Muscles
Leg muscles in an enormous two-footed animal like this dinosaur must have been very large. Those needed to move its small forelimbs would have been less powerful. The muscles attached to each bone of its tail would have been quite small. There are no fossils of dinosaur muscles, but the paleontologist can estimate the size of muscle needed for each action or movement and build up the restoration from this information.

the habits and behavior of the dinosaur—its lifestyle. For this, a mixture of guesswork and experience is used. Some scientists will think that the animal was warm-blooded, others that it was cold-blooded. If it had been warm-blooded, it would have needed a great deal of energy. The heart and the lungs would have had to be very large, like those of an elephant. The lungs may have been small but efficient, with extra air sacs to take as much oxygen as possible from each breath, as do the lungs of modern birds. As a cold-blooded animal, it would have needed only small lungs, more like those of a crocodile.

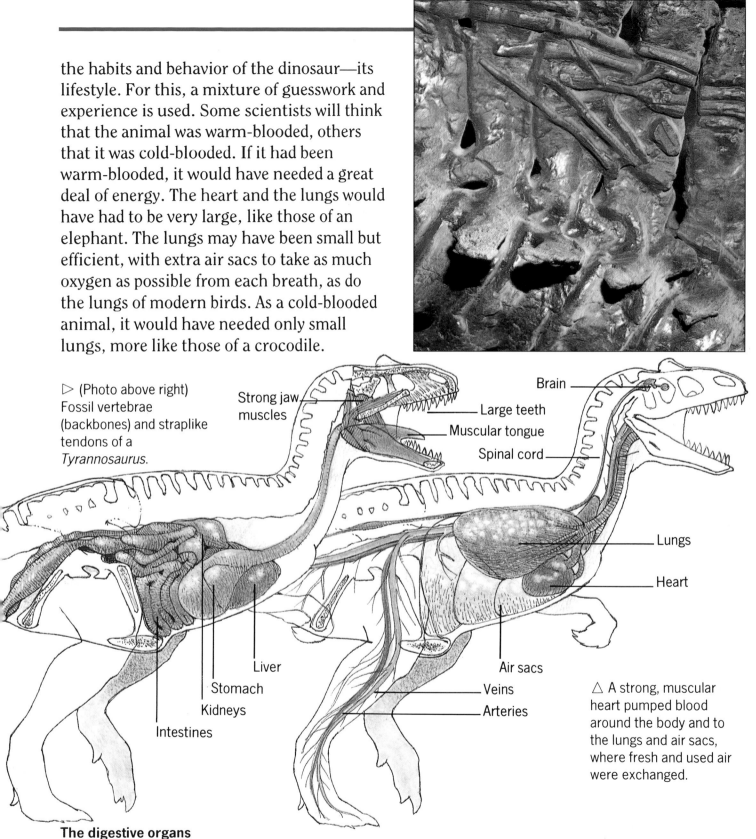

▷ (Photo above right) Fossil vertebrae (backbones) and straplike tendons of a *Tyrannosaurus*.

Strong jaw muscles

Brain

Large teeth

Muscular tongue

Spinal cord

Lungs

Heart

Liver

Stomach

Kidneys

Intestines

Air sacs

Veins

Arteries

△ A strong, muscular heart pumped blood around the body and to the lungs and air sacs, where fresh and used air were exchanged.

The digestive organs

The guts—the stomach and intestines—of a meat-eating dinosaur would have been much smaller than the large complex guts needed to break down and get nutrients from plant food. We know this by looking at present-day meat-eating animals, such as cats and dogs, and plant-eating animals, such as cows and rabbits. Comparison with modern animals is a very important part of restoring and reconstructing a dinosaur's body.

THE COMPLETE DINOSAUR

The final stage in dinosaur restoration probably requires the most imagination—putting the skin on the animal and giving this a color scheme.

For most dinosaurs we have no idea what their skins were like. For a few, we do have skin impressions, which are marks made as skin is pressed into soft ground. The impressions may have been formed as the animal was buried quickly under mud or clay, and the sediments picked up the texture of the skin before it rotted away. Over millions of years, these marks were turned to rock.

Deciding on the skin color is more difficult. There is no evidence available. We believe that dinosaurs had good eyesight and could see colors, so we can be fairly sure that skin color had a part to play in their lives. Big showy bumps on the head, called crests, as well as

Skin color and camouflage
The stripes on this *Allosaurus* restoration are based on those of the tiger. An animal with the same lifestyle may have had a similar color scheme.

sail-like structures on the back, were all probably very colorful. The dinosaurs would have used these as signals. Hunting dinosaurs may have had striped or spotted skins so that they could creep up on their prey unnoticed. Plant-eating animals may well have been camouflaged, with dark colors above and light colors below. Their young may have been striped or dappled so that their colors blended in with sunlit areas and shadows of their nests in the undergrowth. We can only make comparisons with the color schemes of modern animals. What helps today's creatures survive may also have worked for dinosaurs.

Skin texture
The only meat-eating dinosaur for which we have a sample of skin texture is the South American *Carnotaurus*. Most of the skin had a fine scaly texture like a lizard's or snake's, but it also had rows of big scales, like low cones, running the length of the body. *Allosaurus* may have had skin with a similar texture. It is even possible that the smaller meat-eaters were covered with feathers.

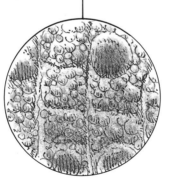

◁ Television-like machines used in medicine to study the insides of the human body can also be used on fossils. They help us to find out about the insides of the dinosaur body structures and so help us construct models, like this one of a dinosaur hatchling.

The mouth
Big meat-eating dinosaurs may have had some form of lips. Evidence of this is the row of little holes along the edge of the jawbone. These may have carried blood vessels to the flesh of the lips.

Claws
Horn is another substance that does not fossilize. The horny claws of a meat-eating dinosaur would have been very much longer than the finger bones.

CONSTRUCTING A LIFE

Even after the body of the dinosaur has been restored, the job of the fossil hunter is only half done. The animal's lifestyle, its fellow creatures, and its surroundings must also be reconstructed in order to create a complete picture of the living beast. Detective work is used to finish this puzzle.

A famous example of a dinosaur puzzle rests in Wyoming. The fossil of a broken *Camarasaurus* skeleton lies exposed on a shelf of sandstone and limestone rock. The softer rock, siltstone, that once covered the dinosaur has been worn away. *Camarasaurus* was a long-necked plant-eater and was common in the area in Late Jurassic times. Among the scattered bones are the broken teeth of the big meat-eating dinosaur *Ceratosaurus* and the small meat-eater *Ornitholestes*. The *Camarasaurus* bones are scored with deep toothmarks, mostly the size of the teeth of *Allosaurus,* another meat-eater.

From these details the paleontologists have worked out a possible story: The *Camarasaurus* lived on a dry plain, since the special mix of limestone and sandstone in the shelf is found only in this type of landscape. One *Camarasaurus* moved away from the main herd and was attacked and killed by an *Allosaurus*. Once the *Allosaurus* had eaten its meal, it moved off. The remains of the *Camarasaurus* were set upon by a group of scavenging *Ceratosaurus*. What was left was finished off by the packs of *Ornitholestes* that had been waiting around like jackals while the bigger animals took the tastiest pieces. Not long afterward a nearby river flooded, covering the plain and the skeleton with silt. This gradually became the siltstone that lay on top of the fossils.

There are other explanations, but the fossil site does show the interaction between the dinosaurs that lived there long ago.

▽ An *Allosaurus* feasts on a young *Camarasaurus*. The clues to this ancient murder lie scattered through the rocks in which the victim is fossilized.

The bones can tell us what kind of animal was killed, and marks on them can reveal what killed it and how.

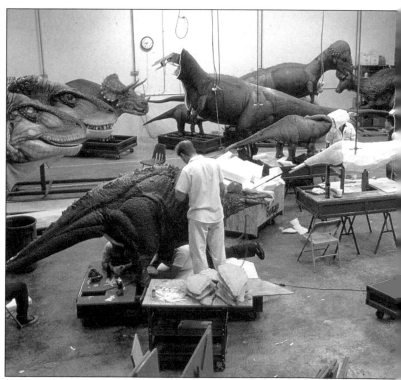

△ Modern museum
reconstructions and
restorations, like this one
at Dallas (Texas) Science
Museum, try to show not
only the animal but also its
surroundings and its
lifestyle. They try to
present the known facts
as a completed jigsaw-
puzzle picture.

▷ Technicians producing
robotic dinosaurs for
display in museums. When
we look at restorations
like these, we can create
in our own minds pictures
of ancient landscapes and
living creatures.

A FASCINATION WITH DINOSAURS

Why do we find dinosaurs so fascinating and fun? It is probably for the same reasons that we like stories of monsters and dragons. We are interested in things that are bizarre and frightening. We enjoy imagining what they were or could be like.

Ever since the fossilized bones were recognized for what they were, and the name *dinosaur* was created, almost 150 years ago, the idea of extinct monsters has gripped people's imaginations and interest. Younger children can pronounce the creatures' names before they can read and write. Dinosaur displays are among the most popular parts of museums. Dinosaurs appear in comic strips, as toys, as badges, as advertizing logos, in the form of cookies, and on postage stamps.

Ever since the Crystal Palace sculptures were built in 1854 there have been dinosaur theme parks. In 1907, concrete dinosaurs were built for Hagenbeck's Zoo in Hamburg, Germany. The most recent development has been the building of full-sized dinosaur models that move.

Dinosaurs have always been popular in the works of literature, from Jules Verne's *Journey to the Center of the Earth* to the most modern science fiction novels like Michael Crichton's *Jurassic Park*. They have also appeared in movies. The spectacular images produced on movie screens lend themselves well to visions of fantastic creatures. *King Kong,* made in 1933, was the dinosaur classic of the first talking motion pictures. Later dinosaur successes included *One Million Years B.C.* and *The Land That Time Forgot*. The movie makers used models, costumed actors, and lizards fitted with horns and sails as animated dinosaurs to give us a glimpse of a world that has long gone.

△ The latest in dinosaur technology—a robot *Triceratops* that can move its head and make sounds. Exhibits like this help us imagine the world of dinosaurs.

◁ The fossil skeleton of a dinosaur lies buried in the ground. It is evidence of a creature that lived more than 140 million years ago when the world was a very different place than it is today.

DO YOU KNOW?

When did the dinosaurs first appear?

The earliest dinosaurs we presently know are *Herrerasaurus* and *Staurikosaurus*. These meat-eaters lived at the start of the Late Triassic Period in South America; they evolved from the crocodile-like thecodonts about 225 million years ago.

When did the dinosaurs die out?

Dinosaurs became extinct at the very end of the Cretaceous Period, about 65 million years ago. For a few million years before this the numbers of dinosaurs had been getting smaller, but then suddenly all these animals, and many others, died out.

How are dinosaurs named?

A dinosaur's proper scientific name (in fact the proper scientific name for all animals) consists of two parts. The first part, the *genus* name, has a capital letter. The second part, the *species* name, does not. Both names are written in italics. Very similar species or kinds of dinosaurs are grouped together in the same genus. That is why we sometimes talk about *Tyrannosaurus rex*. More often we just use the genus name, such as *Tyrannosaurus*.

How many kinds of dinosaurs were there?

It has been estimated that the total number of dinosaur genera (*genera* is the plural of *genus*) that ever lived is between 900 and 1,200. Scientists think that they have discovered about a quarter of the genera that existed.

Which area had the most kinds of dinosaurs?

Triassic, Jurassic, and Cretaceous rocks of western Canada and western United States contain remains of possibly the largest number of different kinds of dinosaurs. They include meat-eaters *Dilophosaurus, Allosaurus,* and *Coelophysis,* long-necked plant-eaters like *Apatosaurus* and *Brachiosaurus,* two-footed plant-eaters such as *Stygimoloch* and *Corythosaurus,* armored *Euoplocephalus* and plated *Stegosaurus,* and the horned *Triceratops.*

Which were the most widely ranging dinosaurs?

Iguanodon, from the United States, Europe, and Mongolia, was likely to have been the most widespread. Other widely distributed dinosaurs included *Brachiosaurus* from Colorado and Tanzania, *Pachyrhinosaurus* from Alberta and Alaska, *Psittacosaurus* from China, Mongolia, and Siberia, and *Chasmosaurus* from Texas and Alberta.

Which were the most southerly dinosaurs?

Scientists have found dinosaur remains in Early Cretaceous rocks of southeastern Australia. These include the armored *Minmi* and two-footed plant-eaters *Fulgurotherium, Leaellynasaura,* and *Atlascopcosaurus.* In Early Cretaceous times this part of Australia lay well within the Antarctic Circle. Dinosaur fossils have also been found in Antarctica, but scientists are not yet sure which species these come from.

Which were the most northerly dinosaurs?

Duckbilled dinosaur remains have been found in Late Cretaceous rocks in Alaska. In Late Cretaceous times this area would have been hundreds of miles farther north than it is today. Footprints like those of *Iguanodon* have been found in Early Cretaceous rocks of the Arctic Islands of Spitzbergen.

Which was the tallest dinosaur?

Ultrasaurus, a long-necked plant-eater like *Brachiosaurus,* could have raised its head to a height of 55 feet above the ground.

Which was the heaviest dinosaur?

As far as we know, *Ultrasaurus* was the heaviest as well as the tallest. In life it would have weighed 100 tons. However, part of a bone belonging to a *Brachiosaurus*-like dinosaur was found in 1987, and this could be from an animal weighing about 130 tons.

Which was the longest dinosaur?

Seismosaurus, or "earthquake reptile," was a long-necked plant-eater like *Diplodocus.* From the incomplete skeleton discovered in 1985, scientists think that the whole animal must have been more than 130 feet long.

Which was the most heavily armored dinosaur?

The ankylosaurs such as *Euoplocephalus* are regarded as the most heavily armored dinosaurs—even their eyelids were armored shutters. The biggest, *Ankylosaurus,* was about 25 feet long. *Saichania* from Mongolia had armor on its belly as well as on its back.

Which dinosaur had the biggest skull?

The ceratopsians—the horned dinosaurs— with their big frills covering their necks, had the biggest skulls. *Torosaurus* had a frilled skull that was 9 feet long—the longest skull known of any land animal ever.

Which dinosaur had the biggest teeth?

Tyrannosaurus had meat-shearing teeth that were more than 6 inches long. These are the biggest dinosaur teeth found.

Which dinosaur had the longest neck?

A complete skeleton of *Mamenchisaurus,* a *Diplodocus*-like long-necked plant-eater from China, has a neck that is 36 feet long, the longest known of any animal. However, in 1987, scientists found the individual bones of a similar but larger animal, and it would have had a neck nearly 50 feet long.

Which dinosaur had the biggest claws?

A Late Cretaceous Mongolian dinosaur called *Therizinosaurus* had the biggest claw that has been discovered. Unfortunately, the arm and hand are the only main parts of the animal that have been found. The arm was about 8 feet long and the bone of at least one claw measured 27½ inches. In life this claw would have been covered with nail, making it much longer. The animal was one of the meat-eating dinosaurs, but some scientists think that it may have eaten only insects.

Which dinosaur had the biggest frill?

Spinosaurus was a meat-eater that may have been as big as *Tyrannosaurus.* On its back it carried a crest that was supported by 5-foot-long bony outgrowths from the backbone.

Which dinosaur had the longest crest?

Parasaurolophus, one of the duckbilled dinosaurs, had a hollow crest that swept back from the skull for a distance of about 6 feet.

Which dinosaur had the longest horns?

The three-horned dinosaur *Triceratops* had a horn on its nose and one over each eye. The bony cores of the eye horns were more than 3 feet long. They must have been much longer in life, when they would have been covered with horny sheaths.

DO YOU KNOW?

Which was the smallest dinosaur?
The little meat-eater *Compsognathus*, with a length of 3 feet and a weight of 5 pounds, is thought of as the smallest dinosaur. Remains of a shorter dinosaur found in Colorado was a two-footed plant-eater related to *Scutellosaurus* but without the armor. It probably weighed about 15 pounds but was only about 2½ feet long.

Which is the smallest baby dinosaur known?
Nests of *Orodromeus*—a plant-eater like *Hypsilophodon*—lie in rocks in Montana. One of the eggs contains an embryo that is 4 inches long. The skeleton of a young *Mussaurus* has been found that is 8 inches long but its tail is missing.

Did any dinosaur climb trees?
Scientists used to believe that *Hypsilophodon* climbed trees. This was because it was built like the modern tree kangaroo and the foot bones seemed to have been adapted to perching. We now know that this was not the case. *Hypsilophodon* was a sprinter.

Which was the most intelligent dinosaur?
What may have been the most intelligent dinosaur was *Troodon* from Late Cretaceous Canada. It was a small meat-eater, and it had a brain as big as that of some of today's birds.

Which was the fastest dinosaur?
A little dinosaur living in Arizona in the Early Jurassic Period left intriguing footprints in the rocks. The animal weighed about 20 pounds and yet made footprints that were about 12 feet apart. Scientists have worked out that the animal must have been running at 40 miles an hour.

Which was the smallest armored dinosaur?
Struthiosaurus from Late Cretaceous eastern Europe was an armored dinosaur that was only about 6 feet long.

Which was the most birdlike dinosaur?
Avimimus, whose name means "bird mimic," had a skeleton that was so birdlike that some scientists think it was covered with feathers and could fly.

Which was the last-surviving plated dinosaur?
Dravidosaurus, a relative of *Stegosaurus*, lived in India in the Late Cretaceous Period. All other stegosaurs died out in Jurassic or Early Cretaceous times. *Dravidosaurus*, which is the only stegosaur known from India, may have lived on there because India was an island at the time, as Australia is now, and there may have been few of its enemies around.

Which was the smallest horned dinosaur?
This was *Microceratops*—"tiny horned face"—from Late Cretaceous China. It was about 30 inches long and was built like *Hypsilophodon*, but it had a tiny nose horn and neck frill.

What was the smallest tyrannosaur?
We think of the tyrannosaurs, such as *Tyrannosaurus*, as being the biggest of the meat-eaters. However, there were smaller types as well. *Nanotyrannus*, from Late Cretaceous Montana, was only 15 feet long.

Which dinosaur had the biggest eyes?
Dromiceiomimus, a relative of *Troodon*, had eyes which were about 3 inches in diameter.

Which dinosaur had the largest eggs?

A long-necked plant-eater, *Hypselosaurus,* whose remains have been found in Late Cretaceous rocks of southern France, had eggs that were about the size of ostrich eggs. They were 12 inches long and 10 inches in diameter. If the eggs had been any bigger, the shells would have been thicker and difficult for the babies to break through.

Which were the longest-lived dinosaurs?

We cannot tell how long each dinosaur lived, but we suspect that the long-necked plant-eaters lived longer than the others. If they were warm-blooded, they may have lived to an age of 100 years. If they were cold-blooded, they may have survived for 200 years or more.

Which dinosaur had the smallest brain?

Stegosaurus had a brain that weighed 2½ ounces. This was only 1/250,000 the weight of its body. (Our brains are about 1/50 the weight of our bodies.)

Which were the most intelligent dinosaurs?

The meat-eaters, particularly small meat-eaters such as *Troodon,* had the biggest brains in relation to their size. Most of the brain capacity, however, was used for sight, hearing, and the other skills needed for hunting.

Which were the most aquatic dinosaurs?

Scientists used to think that the long-necked plant-eaters spent most of their lives in water to help to support their weight and to protect them from the meat-eaters. We now think that they were land-living animals, but occasionally we find their footprints in lake sediments, the layers of mud and sand that settle on the bottom. These show that, in the water, the dinosaurs pulled themselves along by their front feet and changed direction by kicking with the hind feet. This would not have saved them from meat-eaters, as footprints of meat-eaters have been found in lake sediments, too.

Which plant-eating dinosaur had the most teeth?

The duckbilled two-footed plant-eaters, such as *Corythosaurus,* had many hundreds of grinding teeth packed together in each jaw. They formed a filelike surface that was used to tear up the tough plant material on which they fed. The teeth wore out quickly but they were always replaced by new ones.

Which meat-eating dinosaur had the most teeth?

The long-snouted *Baryonyx,* a fish-eater, had twice as many teeth in its jaws as did the other meat-eaters—32 on each side of the lower jaw rather than the usual 16. Many small teeth are better for catching fish than a few big ones.

What is the longest dinosaur name?

So far, *Micropachycephalosaurus,* meaning "little thick-head reptile," with 23 letters, has the longest dinosaur name. It is also one of the smallest dinosaurs. This dome-headed, two-footed plant-eater was about 20 inches long. The shortest dinosaur name is *Minmi* with 5 letters, named after the site in Australia where this armored dinosaur was found.

Which museum has the most types of dinosaur?

The American Museum of Natural History in New York City has the most, with at least 21 different genera of dinosaurs on display.

DO YOU KNOW?

What is the biggest mounted dinosaur skeleton?
The mounted skeleton of *Brachiosaurus* in the Humboldt Museum in Berlin is 72 feet, 9½ inches long. It stands 19 feet, 8 inches high at the shoulders, and the head is carried 39 feet above the ground.

What is the tallest mounted dinosaur skeleton?
A skeleton of *Barosaurus,* a long-necked plant-eater like *Diplodocus,* stands in the American Museum of Natural History in New York City. Rearing up on its hind legs, its head is 55 feet above the floor of the museum.

What is the longest set of fossil footprints?
In Late Jurassic rocks of Colorado there is a run of *Apatosaurus* footprints that goes continuously for a distance of 705 feet.

What country has yielded the most types of dinosaurs?
More genera of dinosaurs have been found in the United States than in any other country—64 at the last count. This is followed closely by Mongolia, with 40, China with 36, Canada with 31, and the United Kingdom with 26.

What is the biggest dinosaur bone discovered so far?
The biggest bone is the solid hip structure of a long-necked plant-eater found in Colorado in 1988, close to where the remains of *Supersaurus* and *Ultrasaurus* were discovered in the late 1970s. This structure, consisting of the hip bones and the vertebrae (backbones) attached to it, measures 6 feet high and 4 feet, 6 inches long, and weighs 1,500 pounds.

Did any dinosaurs survive beyond the Cretaceous Period?
Now and again fossil dinosaur-like teeth are found in rocks that date from after the end of the Cretaceous Period 65 million years ago. Some of the teeth belonged to a kind of land-living crocodile and not to a dinosaur at all. Others are yet unidentified. A number of scientists say that birds evolved from dinosaurs, so although dinosaurs are extinct, their descendants are all around us today!

What is the smallest dinosaur footprint found?
A three-toed footprint less than an inch long, probably from a meat-eater, was found by an amateur collector in the Early Jurassic rocks of Nova Scotia in Canada. The animal that made it must have been about the size of a sparrow.

What was the first mounted dinosaur skeleton?
The plaster cast of the *Hadrosaurus* skeleton mounted by Waterhouse Hawkins under Joseph Leidy's direction in the Academy of Natural Sciences in Philadelphia in 1868 was the first ever on display.

What was the first dinosaur movie?
The first dinosaur movie was a silent cartoon film called *Gertie the Dinosaur,* made by Windsor McCay in 1912. Gertie was, in fact, the first character ever to be designed for a cartoon. The first animated model dinosaur was an *Apatosaurus* filmed in 1914 by Willis O'Brien, who later animated the dinosaurs for *The Lost World* made in 1925 and *King Kong* (1933).

GLOSSARY

algae a very primitive type of plant, such as a seaweed.

ammonites an ancient group of shelled animals, related to modern squid, cuttlefish, and octopuses. They died out at the same time as the dinosaurs.

amphibians vertebrate animals (those with a backbone) that lay their eggs in water but usually spend their adult stage on land. Modern amphibians include frogs and newts.

anatomy the study of the structure of living things—for example, how a dinosaur's bones fitted together, and the size and shape of the various parts of its body.

atmosphere the layer of gases that surrounds the Earth; also known as the air.

beak a horny mouth structure that occurs on birds and some dinosaurs. It is more lightweight than a set of teeth but is used in the same way.

browses feeds on shoots, leaves, and bark of shrubs and trees.

camouflage a natural color scheme or pattern that allows an animal to blend in with its surroundings so that it will not be noticed.

cast the shape that results when the space inside a mold is filled with a muddy sediment that later becomes solid.

cheek pouches folds of skin and muscle at the sides of the mouth that hold food while chewing.

climates the average weather conditions in different parts of the world.

coal a rock made from the remains of ancient plants that were buried and squashed by mud, silt, and sand being laid on top of them.

cold-blooded term used to describe an animal that cannot control the temperature of its body—for example, a fish.

colonization the way in which a new type of plant or animal gradually takes over a new living area.

conifer trees trees that produce seeds in cones—for example, pines, firs, and larches. Their needlelike leaves usually stay on the trees all year.

continents the huge areas of land, or landmasses, on Earth. The modern continents are, in order of size, Asia, Africa, North America, South America, Antarctica, Europe, and Australia.

core the innermost part of the Earth, probably made of iron. The inner core is probably solid and the outer core is liquid.

crest a structure on top of the head, usually for display.

Cretaceous the period of geological time between 146 and 65 million years ago. It was the end of the Age of Dinosaurs.

crust the outer skin of the Earth.

cycad a plant related to the conifers consisting of a stout trunk and a bunch of palmlike leaves.

cycadeoids ancient plants with swollen trunks that resembled the modern cycads.

deposit in geology, rock material such as sand and pebbles laid down in an area after having been carried from elsewhere by rivers, wind, glaciers, or the sea.

digest to break down food in the stomach and intestines into a form that can be absorbed and used by the body.

environments the total of the living conditions of animals, including the landscape, the climate, the plants growing in the area, and all the other animals that live all around.

evolved changed, over many generations, to produce a new species.

fangs long pointed teeth.

ferns nonflowering plants with finely divided leaves known as fronds.

fiberglass glass in the form of very fine strands. When mixed with gluelike materials, it forms a very tough and lightweight substance.

flash flood a sudden rush of water down a river valley following rainfall in nearby mountains.

fossilized turned into fossils.

fossils parts or traces of once-living plants or animals that are preserved in the rocks.

fronds the finely divided leaves of fern plants.

geography the study of the appearance, formation, and changes to the land, sea, and air on Earth. A major branch of geography is geology, the science of rocks, minerals and fossils.

ginkgoes trees that look like conifers but with leaves that are shed in the fall. There is only one living species, the Maidenhair tree.

Gondwana the southern section of the ancient continent of Pangaea, consisting of what is now South America, Africa, India, Australia, and Antarctica.

grazed to have eaten low-growing plants. Modern grazers eat grass and include sheep, goats, many antelope, and cattle.

greenhouse effect a heating up of the Earth's surface because a change in the makeup of the atmosphere stops the warmth from the ground from escaping into space.

growth rings rings of bone or wood produced as an animal or a tree grows. Animals and plants may grow at different speeds at various times of the year, and this is seen as layers of light and dark colors in the bone or wood.

hatchling an animal that is newly hatched from its egg.

herbivores plant-eating animals.

hooves very tough and heavy toenails built to take the weight of an animal.

horn a tough, shiny substance made of the same chemical material as hair, and often formed as a protective covering on some part of an animal. The name is also used for a pointed structure covered with horn.

horsetail plants plants, related to ferns, with sprays of green branches along an upright stem and tiny leaves.

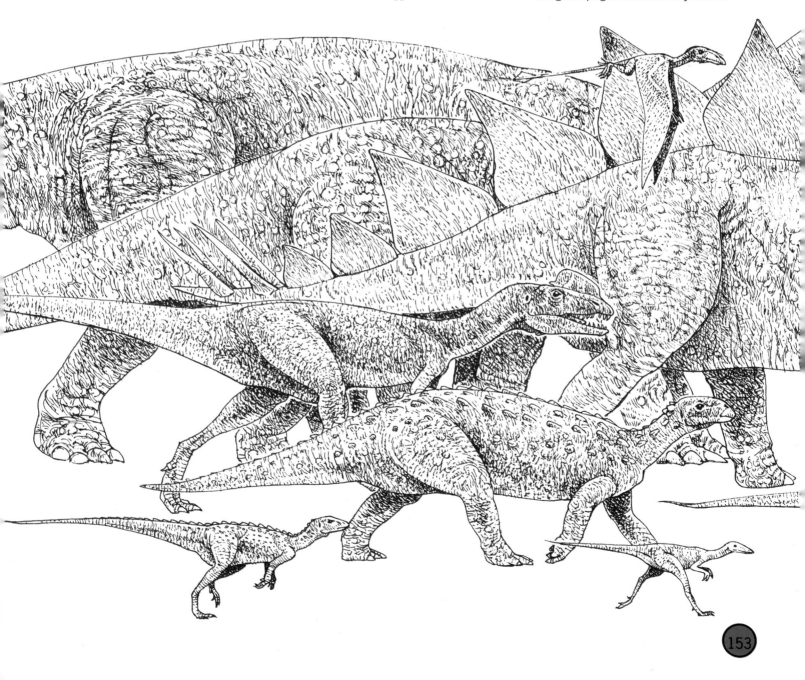

ichthyosaurs swimming reptiles of Triassic, Jurassic, and Cretaceous times that were so adapted to life in the water that they looked like modern dolphins.

impression a mark or print in the surface of the ground or a rock made by something pressing against or in it.

intestines the parts of the food canal beyond the stomach from which the nutrients are absorbed into the blood for use by the cells and tissues of the body.

Jurassic the period of geological time between 208 and 146 million years ago. It is the middle period of the Age of Dinosaurs.

Laurasia the northern section of Pangaea, consisting of what is now North America, Europe, and most of Asia.

lifespans the lengths of time animals live.

limestone a rock made up mainly of the mineral calcite. Some limestones are formed from the calcite of shells of sea animals that died long ago and were buried on the sea bed.

lungfish fish that have lungs as well as gills and so can breathe air. They can survive droughts or live in stagnant waters.

mammal-like reptile a member of a group of reptiles that were common in the Permian Period, before dinosaurs evolved. They developed all kinds of mammal-like features such as teeth of different sizes. They eventually evolved into the mammals themselves.

mammals vertebrate (backboned) animals that produce live young and feed them on milk. Modern mammals include cats, dogs, mice, rabbits, whales, monkeys, and ourselves.

mantle the stony layer that makes up the bulk of the Earth. It is solid but with a soft layer near the top.

meteorite a lump of rock from space that falls to Earth.

migrated moved from place to place as conditions changed to find new sources of food or shelter or to mate and bring up young.

minerals substances formed naturally in the ground of which all rocks are made. They include mixtures of elements such as iron, aluminum, potassium, carbon, silicon, oxygen, and hydrogen.

molds hollow containers, each having the shape of a particular object into which a liquid is poured. When the liquid hardens, it takes the object's shape. The copy of the object is known as a cast.

molecules the smallest particles of chemical compounds formed by the joining together of atoms, the building units of all matter.

Ornithischia the bird-hipped dinosaurs, including the two-footed plant-eaters, the plated dinosaurs, the armored dinosaurs, and the horned dinosaurs.

ornithopod a two-footed plant-eating dinosaur, such as *Iguanodon*.

paleontologist a person who studies paleontology, the science of living things in earlier times as known from the examination of fossils.

Pangaea the name given to the supercontinent that once existed in which all the continental masses of the Earth were joined together.

Permian the period of geological time between 290 and 245 million years ago. The time when the reptiles were taking over from the amphibians and the period immediately before dinosaurs appeared.

plaster of Paris a mixture of fine powder and water that sets hard. It is used to make casts in pottery and also to protect a person's broken bones until they have healed.

plesiosaurs swimming reptiles from the Age of Dinosaurs that had squat bodies, paddles as limbs, and either long necks and small heads or short necks and big heads.

predators meat-eating animals that hunt and kill other animals for food.

prehistoric in ancient times; before written historical records.

prey an animal that is hunted and eaten by a predator.

pterosaur a member of a group of flying reptiles, related to the dinosaurs, that flew using wings of skin during the Triassic, Jurassic, and Cretaceous periods.

quicksand an area of wet sand that may become almost liquid when stepped on. Swallows up anything that walks on it.

reconstruction the skeleton of an animal rebuilt from its bones or casts of the bones.

reptiles cold-blooded vertebrate animals that reproduce by laying hard-shelled or leathery eggs on land. Snakes, lizards, turtles, terrapins, and crocodiles are modern types of reptiles.

restoration a picture or a model of an animal as it appeared in life. This may include showing the surroundings of the animal.

sandstone a rock formed from sand particles cemented together.

Saurischia the lizard-hipped dinosaurs, including the meat-eaters and the long-necked plant-eaters.

sauropod a long-necked plant-eating dinosaur, such as *Apatosaurus*.

scales in reptiles, small leaves of horn that form part of the outer covering.

scavenger a meat-eating animal that does not make its own kills but eats the bodies of other animals already dead.

sediment tiny pieces of soil, earth, or rock—for example, grains of sand or specks of mud that are deposited at the bottom of the sea or on a river bed.

silt a sediment that is finer than sand but coarser or rougher than mud.

siltstone rock formed from silt particles cemented together by pressure from layers of more sediment from above.

species a collection of animals, or any living things, in which individuals look like one another and can breed with each other to produce young. Breeding, reproduction, and mating are all terms to describe the process by which individuals make more of their species.

tendons tough pieces of animal tissue that attach the muscles to the bones.

theropod a meat-eating dinosaur, such as *Tyrannosaurus*.

tree ferns plants of the fern family that grow to 80 feet or more in height. There are only a few living species, but they were plentiful at the beginning of the Age of Dinosaurs.

Triassic the period of geological time between 245 and 208 million years ago. The dinosaurs first evolved in the Triassic Period.

vertebrates animals that have a backbone. This includes the fish, amphibians, reptiles, birds, and mammals. As mammals, we are also vertebrates.

vocal cords the structures in the throat of many vertebrates that vibrate and produce a noise as air passes over them.

voice box the structure in the throat of an animal in which the voice is produced. This usually contains the vocal cords.

warm-blooded term used to describe an animal that can regulate its own body temperature—for example, a mammal or a bird.

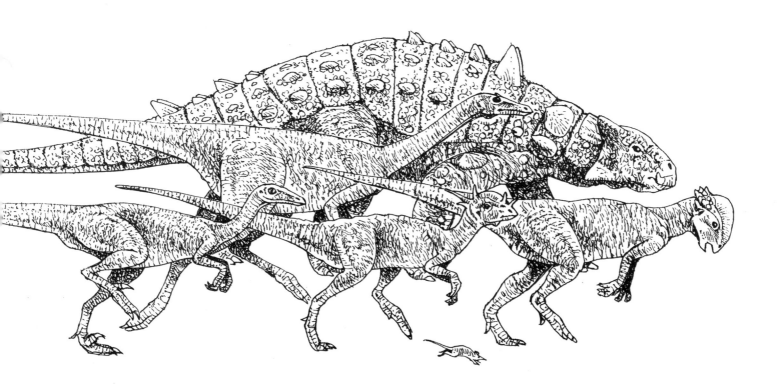

INDEX

Numbers in ordinary type refer to text; numbers in **bold** refer to captions; numbers in *italic* refer to illustration labels or chart annotation.

ACKNOWLEDGMENTS

Picture credits
Pages 18/19 C.A. Henley/Biofotos. 44 J.B. Davidson/Survival Anglia. 49 R. Van Nostrand/Frank Lane Photo Agency. 51 Jeff Foott/Survival Anglia. 65 Udo Hirsch/Bruce Coleman Limited. 67 K.G. Preston-Mafham/Premaphotos Wildlife. 68 Keith and Liz Laidler/Ardea London Limited. 71,73 K.G. Preston-Mafham/ Premaphotos Wildlife. 75 J.J. Brooks/Aquila Photographics. 82 Partridge Films Ltd/Oxford Scientific Films. 85 Michael Fogden/Oxford Scientific Films. 86 Hans Reinhard/Bruce Coleman Limited. 88 Bob Langrish/Frank Lane Photo Agency. 93 Heather Angel. 96/97 Soames Summerhays/Biofotos. 99 K.G. Preston-Mafham/Premaphotos Wildlife. 101 A. Christiansen/Frank Lane Photo Agency. 105 Robert Maier/Aquila Photographics. 105 Adrian Warren/Ardea London Limited. 107 Joan Root/Survival Anglia. 109 M. Lane/Aquila Photographics. 112 Hans Reinhard/Bruce Coleman Limited. 115 John Downer/Oxford Scientific Films. 124 Ann Ronan Picture Library. 125 The Natural History Museum, London. 126 Dr. Pat Morris. 127 The Natural History Museum, London. 128,129 Department of Paleontology, Royal Belgian Institute of Natural Sciences, Brussels. 131 (top and right) Yale Peabody Museum of Natural History. 131 (bottom left) Mary Evans Picture Library. 134,135 The Natural History Museum, London. 136,137 The Natural History Museum, London. 139 Dr. Pat Morris. 141 John Cancalosi/Bruce Coleman Limited. 143 (both) Peter Menzel/Science Photo Library. 144/145 The Natural History Museum, London. 145 The Natural History Museum, London.

Artwork credits
Chris Forsey: pages 1, 4-7, 22-31, 34-35, 62-63, 90-91, 92-93, 98-99, 102-109, 113, 118-119, 120-127. James G. Robins: pages 8-13, 18-19, 20-21, 32-33, 94-95, 110-111, 128-129, 130, 134, 135, 136-141, 151-156. Dennys Ovenden: cover and pages 20-21, 33, 100, 114-115, 142-143. Hayward Art Group: pages 14-15, 116-117, 132-133 and all diagrammatic artwork. Steve Kirk: all major color illustrations on pages 3, 36-61, 64-89.